CREATING CHARACTERS
Let Them Whisper Their Secrets

Marisa D'Vari

Published by Michael Wiese Productions
11288 Ventura Blvd, Suite 621
Studio City CA 91604
Tel. (818) 379-8799
Fax (818) 986-3408
mw@mwp.com
www.mwp.com

Cover Design: Michael Wiese Productions
Layout: Gina Mansfield
Editor: Arthur G. Insana

Printed by McNaughton & Gunn, Inc., Saline, Michigan
Manufactured in the United States of America

Library of Congress Cataloging-in-Publication Data
D'Vari, Marisa.
    Creating characters : let them whisper their secrets / Marisa D'Vari.
        p. cm.
    Includes bibliographical references.
    ISBN 0-941188-97-3
    1. Motion picture authorship. 2. Characters and characteristics in
literature. I. Title.
    PN1996.D367 2005
    808'.066791--dc22

2004012796

"Aspiring authors everywhere owe Marisa D'Vari a thank-you note. *Creating Characters* shines a much-needed spotlight on the realities of writing for both Manhattan publishers and Hollywood studios."
> — **Jeremiah Healy**, author of *Spiral, The Only Good Lawyer*, and 15 other mystery novels.

"An invaluable guidebook for authors and screenwriters who may be looking for that crucial but mysterious key that makes fictional characters spring to life."
> — **John Blumenthal**, author of *Millard Fillmore, Mon Amour*

"A wonderful book, as consoling as it is insightful. It belongs on every writer's night-table."
> — **Dennis Palumbo**, psychotherapist and author, *Writing from the Inside Out*

"Before putting pen to paper, read *Creating Characters*. Marisa D'Vari gives writers a practical foundation for character development with tools and exercises that engage writers and result in fully formed 'people' who live and breathe."
> — **Jennifer O'Connell**, author of *Bachelorette #1*

"This book is an invaluable treasure trove of advice. Whether you are a screenwriter or a novelist, a few afternoons reading, pencil in hand, will give you insight and ideas that are sure to give your characters interesting edges, contours, heart, soul, and guts."
> — **M. J. Rose**, author of *Sheet Music, The Halo Effect, Flesh Tones*

"In *Creating Characters*, Marisa D'Vari has pulled together a fascinating array of tools for psychological and spiritual insight, teamed up with practical exercises and advice for dealing with publishers and producers. She calls her method the More-Personality system, and her stylish writing shows more personality than many novels. Both new and experienced writers can get fresh ideas from this book."
> — **Toni L. P. Kelner**, author of *Wed and Buried*

"*Creating Characters* is an excellent book for writers interested in analyzing their characters and deciding what sort of character would fit best into a plot. Marisa D'Vari's experience with screenwriting and grasp of theory result in highly useful advice."
> — **Sarah Smith**, best-selling author of *Chasing Shakespeares, The Vanished Child, The Knowledge of Water*

"Filled with insider secrets, *Creating Characters* empowers you with tools, tips, and techniques to fashion vibrant personalities which engage your audience. The underpinning is a personality typology Marisa D'Vari developed and artfully illuminates with many examples from popular culture."
> — **Dr. David Chananie**, *Writer's Digest* award-winning author of *Not Yet At Ease: Photographs of America's Continuing Engagement With the Vietnam War*

Dedication

Today's films burst with dynamic, mesmerizing characters made dazzling by top screenwriters and great looking actors, yet few movie stars have the brilliance, wit, and incredibly gorgeous looks of Ron D'Vari.

Thanks, Ron, for inspiring and supporting this book.

Special Thanks to Ken Atchity

In 1994, I heard a fellow writer raving about *A Writer's Time*, by Ken Atchity. Intrigued, I bought a copy and read it three times before putting it down. It was the first time I had considered the role of the subconscious mind in the writing process.

Thus, I began my decade long journey into the power of the subconscious mind. My first book, *Script Magic: Subconscious Techniques to Conquer Writer's Block* was released in 2000 and, from the e-mails and letters received, empowered screenwriters as Ken Atchity had empowered me.

In this book, *Creating Characters: Let Them Whisper Their Secrets*, Ken Atchity has gone out of his way to make it a success, endorsing it with an introduction and arranging for me to interview his influential contacts.

Thank you, Ken, for your generosity with this book and for bringing the power of the subconscious mind into the limelight.

Warm Acknowledgements

Michael Wiese, publisher, Ken Lee, VP of MWP, and Michele Chong, thanks so much for your efforts!

To my agent, Colleen Mohyde, you are the best!

Many thanks to the generous screenwriters, story analysts, authors, and experts who gave the most eye-opening interviews any writer can hope for. Very appreciative to Allison Burnett, John Blumenthal, Keith Davis, Beverly Gray, Rosemary Ellen Guiley, Ph.D., Professor Lew Hunter, Dr. Dennis Palumbo, David Tausik, and Chris Vogler.

To Jane Sindell, for being the best first boss anyone could have. And thanks to Mike Medavoy for inspiring leadership when I was at TriStar Films.

Editors Lucia Macro, Anna Genoese, and Kate Duffy, thanks for revealing insider publishing secrets!

Also, much gratitude to Michael Kuciak of Atchity Entertainment International for his assistance… and to fellow writers Kate Flora, MJ Rose, Sarah Smith, Kathryn Lance, G. Miki Hayden, Jennifer O'Connell, MJ Schirmer, Bobbye Terry, and Bill Neugent.

Troy Browning, Becky Sue Epstein, and Jeremiah Healy, much appreciation!

Ditto to Bill Corcoron, Janet Lang, and Mr. Lloyd Sheldon Johnson who saw this success – and more!

Finally, much appreciation to Gabriele Meiringer of the Writers Store and the staff at Book Soup on L.A.'s Sunset Strip!

Table of Contents

Foreword

By Dr. Kenneth Atchity

Character is the essence of drama, the primary mechanism from which compelling action arises to hold audiences in thrall. In all media, from epic to play to novel to screenplay, great dramatists have been applauded for their ability to create memorable characters: Hektor bidding farewell to his wife and infant son on the wall of Troy in Homer's *Iliad*; Lear, tossing away a kingdom to test the meaning and limits of love; Ahab, willing to risk his life and the lives of his men to avenge himself against Moby Dick; or Kane, dancing through hubris to self destruction in Orson Welles' masterpiece.

The creation of memorable characters is both the most elusive and the simplest task of the dramatist — the act in which he or she melds the workings of conscious craft and unconscious inspiration.

How is a dramatic character "born?" Like Athena from the head of Zeus, a character is born straight from the writer's head — without benefit or burden of the tedious normal process of childhood and adolescence.

But how does a writer create a character full-blown? There are probably as many answers to this question as there are storytellers, but the formula I keep coming back to is, "What would happen if a character like this found himself involved in a situation like that?" What would happen if a character who trusts his father above all but loves his mother more found out that his father may have been murdered with her cooperation? Explore this in a dark mood, and you have Shakespeare's Hamlet. *Splash* was created from the question, "What would happen if a man who glimpsed a mermaid long ago and never stopped thinking about her discovered she had left the sea to find him because she'd never stopped thinking about him?"

William Faulkner's process was to allow a character to haunt him, to incarnate in his mind from repeated visitations. Instead of trying to write something the first time he glimpsed the character, he ignored it until it kept coming back to pester him. Then he began asking questions, questions based on observation of the character's image in his mind: a young girl, with muddy underpants and unscraped knees, up a tree, watching a funeral through the window of a big house:

Why were her pants muddy?

Why was she up this tree?

Why were her knees unscraped?

Why was she looking in on the funeral from outside?

Whose funeral was it?

By the time he'd listed these, and more, questions, he had already begun discovering answers. When he had enough answers, he felt compelled to begin writing — in this case, *The Sound and the Fury*, from the character of Candace.

In editing and publishing *DreamWorks* with my colleague Marsha Kinder, we discovered that artists in all genres regularly create the condition for easy passage between the external real world and the internal world of dreams. That two-way passage, the well-trod path of both storyteller and shaman, is symbolized in

Virgil's *Aeneid* by "the gates of horn and ivory"; and in Miguel de Cervantes' *Don Quixote de la Mancha* by the "cave of the Montesinos."

The mysterious imagination, that seat of creativity that lies somewhere between the conscious and unconscious mind, is the infinite font from which the most memorable fictional characters spring. Productive writers have learned tricks to awaken the imagination, to incite it to do its job.

This book is a well-organized sleight-of-hand, a guide to tricking your imagination into creative action. The author includes concrete examples of how successful screenwriters and authors have accessed their dream factory, and gives practical step-by-step advice about how you can do it, too. Her suggestions for "channeling your characters via dialogue" or taking your character to "a goal-setting workshop" are just two of the many tricks she suggests to open that passage to the world of the imagination whence characters are born.

The More-Personality™ system, which D'Vari developed in "clinical" encounters with writers over the years, is an innovative tool for jump-starting characterization when you're faced with a blank page, as well as an instrument to sharpen characterization, add additional depth, nuance, and characteristics, assist with discovering a character's voice, discover potential conflicts between characters; and finally, a time-saving checklist to ensure that all characters in your story are diverse enough to draw and maintain an audience's interest. It can help you determine what the "this" is in the formula "a character like this."

Some writers plot their stories first, and then create characters to fit their stories' demands. In this scenario, the More-Personality can help them quickly add the flesh of back story to the characters' skeletons. Other writers find their characters through dreams, or via intriguing people they meet, see, or read about and can use the More-Personality system to balance their characters and see their characters in a more objective light.

In my own books on writing, *A Writer's Time: A Guide to the Creative Process, from Vision through Revision, How to Publish Your Novel,* and *Writing Treatments That Sell: How to Create and Market Your Story Ideas to the Motion Picture and TV Industry,* I outline the four dynamic elements from which fictional characters are constructed: motivation, mission, obstacles, and change. If these four elements are the skeleton of created character, D'Vari's elements are the flesh that makes your characters appear to be real (when, in fact, they're not).

D'Vari developed this system from her knowledge of the Enneagram, Jungian personality types, the Myers-Briggs system, and the development practices of the Hollywood studios. You'll enjoy the self-quiz she's constructed to let you figure out your own type, as well as the type of your characters, which will help you flesh them out and make them seem real. She introduces the

M = Mover (who moves fast, wants information fast, uses action oriented words)
O = Observer (who's analytical by nature)
R = Relater (who's "people" oriented)
E = Energizer (who's a storyteller, colorful, vibrant, outgoing)

She explains each of the four types in exemplary detail, using celebrity personalities and screen roles for clear illustration. She includes exercises that allow writers to dig deep into their characters, as well as unique personality quirks associated with each type.

Using her system, you'll be able to:
  ❖ Understand how your character relates to other personality types in the story;

❖ Ensure that you have a realistic sprinkling of different types in your story;

❖ Understand your character's phobias and preferences, by his type;

❖ Plot a more realistic developmental pathway to your character's goals;

❖ Create more realistic obstructions to your character's goal; and

❖ Devise more credible dialogue, as your character will speak by type.

Of course, the point of any system is to get the motor running. You'll begin creating your own shortcuts, your own exceptions, your own way of doings things the minute you put her excellent advice into action. It's all about getting rid of writer's block and getting your characters up and running.

What writers mean when they say, "My characters talk to me," is that they've given them a chance to take dramatic shape in their minds by bringing the elements within each character that makes that character conflicted, and therefore dramatically involving, into focus. When a character is *not* focused, it lies inertly on the page like so many words. When it *is* focused, by having its external mission and internal conflict clear cut and reflected in the way it moves, speaks, and acts — audiences say, "Her characters come alive."

That's the goal of this book: to help you create characters who come alive.

❖❖❖❖❖

Atchity (Yale Ph.D.) is a writer-producer-literary manager-professor-editor, whose Story Merchant companies (*www.thestorymerchant.com*) are Atchity Entertainment International (*www.aeionline.com*, for writers "ready for prime time"), The Writers Lifeline (*www.thewriterslifeline.com*, for writers "not yet ready for prime time), and The Creative Media Group for story-tellers who've passed beyond prime time into becoming international brands. His clients, among them bestselling authors and screenwriters, include former Minnesota Governor Jesse Ventura, Ripley's Believe-It-Or-Not!, Beyond Comics, and The Learning Annex.

Introduction

Encouraging Characters to Whisper Their Secrets

Do you remember the last time a friend, co-worker, or Starbucks stranger volunteered intimate personal information about themselves, *out of the blue*?

Recently, a prominent man whispered that his wife was addicted to sexy La Perla lingerie, he gambled in Vegas "because life was all about chance," and endured horrific nightmares of being sucked dry by a vampire — all within 10 minutes of meeting him.

At a staid financial conference, a bland investment manager in a navy blazer and khaki pants casually revealed he slit the throat of a famous Colombian drug war lord in cold blood while working as an American spy.

Demure and sophisticated in her classy St. John suit, a respected female physician volunteered she regularly slept with cabana boys when attending upscale medical conferences at fancy tropical resorts.

Surprise, shock, fascination – *yes, I wanted to hear more.*

How many times have you sat down with your own fictional characters, and waited patiently... *almost too patiently*, for them to reveal as much juicy information as loose-lipped strangers tell us over dry Ketel One Martinis and salted peanuts?

Dull, lackluster characterization is why 97% of scripts and novels are rejected in both Hollywood and the publishing industry. Compelling characters shock, surprise, delight, fascinate, and *vibrate color and energy* with each line of dialogue and every action they take.

So, what are the secrets to creating compelling characters who make buyers jump up and scream *"yes!"*

Ask a dozen executives to define "good characterization" and you are likely to get a shrug and "I'll know it when I see it" response.

This book offers a lively and exciting catalog of creative writing techniques you can employ to create memorable and authentic characters. First, you will discover how to jump-start your story with the More-Personality system, which enables you to quickly and easily brainstorm an endless variety of character traits that correspond to your character's personality style. You will also discover the right mix of personality styles for your story, and how to use personality styles to maximize conflict between characters and in the story.

Second, you will learn how to harness the power of dreams to add depth and dimension to your characters. Horror author Stephen King depends on dreams to fuel his writing. Ingmar Bergman put his dream of four women in mourning in *Cries and Whispers*, and a coffin dream in *Wild Strawberries*. The rock musician Sting based an entire break-out album on his dream.

Third, you will receive uncensored advice from a dozen screenwriters and novelists who've kept their characterization secrets to themselves — until now! You will be given a virtual visit to a studio story department, offered a glimpse of what analysts look for as they write "studio coverage" on your book or screenplay, and learn the "do's" and "don'ts" that can alienate readers before they reach page 10 of your script or book.

In the course of this book, I refer to these initial readers or screeners as "gatekeepers." We will discuss them at length in Chapter 7, where both successful writers and experienced gate-keepers give you solid advice on "best practices" to implement in order to excite people about your material and get your project "bumped" to the next level.

Tools you will need for the many exercises in the book include a notebook (which is to be carried with you at all times), an open mind, and the willingness to expand your powers of observation.

◆ CHAPTER ONE ◆

CREATING RICHER CHARACTERS THROUGH PERSONALITY TYPES

Did you ever see a film or read a book, and strongly feel you have met the character before? Or maybe you have met someone new who seems eerily familiar and you thought: *"I better be wary of him – I've met his type before!"*

Scientists are discovering more about the behaviour of the human brain every day, including the fact that we take in over one hundred separate messages about a new person we meet *every second*. The process takes place on a subconscious level in the amygdala part of our brain, and dates back to the "friend or foe" caveman days when our ancestors had to immediately size up a stranger to see if he was a threat or potential helpmate.

Today, this part of the brain still scans new people and new situations for information that will help us survive. This is why we often immediately like or dislike people before they even open their mouths, as they remind us of people in the past with whom we have had good or negative experiences.

Researchers have discovered that certain physical traits and personalities are universally likeable. We can see this in actresses such as Goldie Hawn and Cameron Diaz, two blonde, kooky actresses of a similar type who seem safe, funny, and familiar.

Hit TV shows, such as *Friends*, are peopled with character types who seem familiar, likeable, and whom we wish were our friends in reality. This is exactly the element which makes these shows so popular and the reason why top cast members make more than a million dollars a week. Savvy advertisers know that the audience perceives its favorite TV characters to be intimate friends, and who better than a cool, intimate friend to sell us toothpaste?

Due to the short length of the sit-com format, TV casting directors know the actors have only a few seconds to make a positive impression. Audiences make snap assessments, and if personality had to be revealed through the dialogue and plot, an audience would have flipped the channel. Therefore, cast members must radiate likeability and cues to their personality type in a single glance.

Even though your goal is to write screenplays and novels, and thus will have the time to develop your character's personality through dialogue and behavior, discovering the art of personality typecasting will get you thinking about your protagonist, and how he relates to the other character types in your work, in an entirely new way.

You may wonder why understanding the history and application of personality typecasting is important to writers, and how you can use this technique. Here are three key ways to use personality typecasting in your work.

In the first scenario, you have a plot or story idea, but no characters. Since the protagonist in most screenplays and novels is either an "Energizer character" or a "Mover character," you will be able to learn the personality characteristics of both types, and decide which type you want to feature, along with their characteristics.

In the second scenario, you know the character in your screenplay or novel that needs to be "fleshed out." Use what you will come to learn as the More-Personality™ system to decide on their personality types, and again, select the appropriate behavior patterns that correspond to those styles.

In the third scenario, you know the story and the character(s), and even may have written a first draft. The challenge is that there isn't enough friction between the characters, or action to drive the plot. Again, you can use the More-Personality system to find potential areas where your characters will clash and thus add more story dynamics.

Just so you know where we are headed, the four basic styles of the More-Personality system are listed below:

Mover – brash, "Type A" personality, result driven, fast moving & thinking;
Observer – factual, observant, often insecure, focused on detail, aloof;
Relater – encourages & motivates others, service oriented, likes human contact;
Energizer – storyteller, confident, ambitious, likeable, charming, quick thinking;

With this system, writers can:

❖ Understand how your character relates to other personality types in the story;
❖ Ensure that you have a realistic sprinkling of different types in your story;
❖ Understand your character's phobias and preferences, by his type;
❖ Plot a more realistic developmental pathway to your character's goals;
❖ Create more realistic obstructions to your character's goal;
❖ Devise more credible dialogue as your character will speak by type.

As you know, the objective of screenplays and novels is to show a character's growth and development from the beginning of a story to its conclusion. In the best of all circumstances, the character (through his experience or journey) is in a better situation. Even if the quest ends in death (as it did in the film *Gladiator*) the character achieved his heroic objective.

Many authors are not aware that their characters even have specific types, let alone what those types may be. As you will read in the coming pages, it is remarkably easy to find out which of the four types best fits your character. Many individuals and characters fit into two overlapping categories, which is fine. Yet rarely would you find any individual or character fitting into more than three categories, for it would mark the individual as something of a schizophrenic and the character as unbelievable.

The More-Personality system is also a powerful tool to:

❖ Learn "all" your character's traits (shared by similar types);
❖ Discover the "best and worst" aspects of each individual type;
❖ Find people or situations this specific type finds attractive;
❖ Help you brainstorm appropriate scenes/situations for your characters;
❖ Learn your characters' histories;
❖ Learn the "types" of friends your characters seek to acquire;
❖ Discover how the personalities of these friends can impact your character;
❖ Generate the best "significant other" your character can have to achieve his goal;
❖ Help you see the relationships between characters;
❖ Quickly create characters that both block a character from his goal and push him toward it;
❖ Allow you to learn how your character is impacted by interactions of each of the four character types;

Now before we delve too deeply into the More-Personality system and illustrate the many ways you can use it to craft more dynamic characters, let's take a look at the way personality typecasting developed.

History of Personality Typecasting

At some point in your life, you must have been struck by how similar a new acquaintance is to a good friend, or someone you've known in the past. These same musings were also experienced by an ancient civilization that created a system called the Enneagram to explain this phenomenon.

Exact origins of this civilization are not exactly known, but the system is believed to originate in ancient Greece or the Middle East over 3,000 years ago.

Ennea is the Greek word for nine, so Enneagram (pronounced any a-gram) is a Greek word meaning "nine diagrams." Thus, the Enneagram details nine very specific types of personality styles represented by a circle containing a nine-pointed star-like shape.

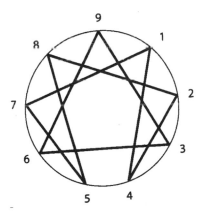

Model of the Enneagram

Today, the Enneagram personality system is taught by a wide variety of speakers and authors, many of whom assign their own word to represent the personality style of each of the nine types. So while the personality characteristics associated with each of the nine types remain consistent, every author/speaker might call "Type 3" by a name of his or her own choosing.

Basically, the Enneagram and other personality typecasting systems feel that the same "types" have the same basic motivations and view the world in the same fundamental ways. Even though the Enneagram is partly based on the zodiac, your personality type is not contingent upon when you were born. Rather, it is the collective personality traits that are attributable to a specific type.

Let us use a casual friend named John as an example. When I first delved into the Enneagram, I was unsure if John was a Type 2 (Helper) or Type 4 (Romantic).

Types 2s are motivated by the need to be loved, valued, and appreciated. Traditionally, they embody the female ideal of being "nurturers." Yet I noticed depression, moodiness, and other qualities in John that suggested he was a Type 4 (Romantic). When I verbalized this to him, he told me that others who have studied the Enneagram have expressed the same confusion. Now experienced with the Enneagram, I know John is a Type 4 (Romantic), so realize that your first guess may be accurate, but the more you come to know the Enneagram, the more accurate you can become.

Students of the Enneagram who wish to find their types are first advised to find their "centers." For example, authors Renee Baron and Elizabeth Wagele in *The Enneagram Made Easy* state that the heart (image), or feeling center includes Type 2 (helpers), Type 3 (Achievers), and Type 4 (Romantics).

The head or thinking center (fear) includes Type 5 (Observers), Type 6 (Questioners), and Type 7 (Adventurers).

The gut or instinctive center (anger) includes Type 8 (Asserters), Type 9 (Peacemakers), and Type 1 (Perfectionists).

The Enneagram is quite rich when it comes to typing individuals, but of limited use to writers. First, the nine basic types, with each type having nine variations, is overkill as far as a characterization tool is concerned. Individuals would have to spend several months studying the system to find their own types, aside from the type of each character in their screenplays or books.

Second, as you saw from my example with John, if it takes months for a scholar to decide if John is a Type 2 or Type 4, how would the viewing or reading audiences be able to accurately "type" your characters when they first meet them? Even making the likely assumption that your audience has never heard of the Enneagram, using the Enneagram to type an individual leaves too much room for speculation.

Clearly, another personality typing system is in order.

Hippocrates and the Four Temperament Styles
Hippocrates, called "the father of modern medicine," was born in Greece in 460 B.C. Despite his moniker, when he was born people had no knowledge of medicine and believed that humans suffered from diseases because of supernatural causes such as the action of unfriendly spirits, ghosts, and demons, or from witchcraft.

Hippocrates did not believe in any of the superstitious explanations given for the ailments of the human body, nor did he believe in miraculous cures. He conducted experiments to understand the workings of the human body and formed a 10-volume encyclopedia of medicine and surgery as known in his day.

In the course of his work, Hippocrates quickly became fascinated with the way bodily fluids, in his mind, corresponded with personality types. He concluded that our behavior style was determined genetically at birth rather than from external influences such as astrology or birth order, and identified the physiology of each of the four temperament styles based on the "humours" of the body.

To wit, Hippocrates decried that we are born with a combination of four genetic influences: Choleric (Worker), Sanguine (Talker), Phlegmatic (Watcher) and Melancholy (Thinker).

According to Hippocrates, the extroverted Choleric (Worker) was short-tempered and ill-natured, but was action-oriented. The extroverted Sanguine (Talker) was cheerful, outgoing, and optimistic, yet lacked organizational skills. The introverted Phlegmatic (Watcher) was slow and sluggish, but was reliable under pressure. The introverted Melancholy (Thinker) was deep, sad, and depressive, but also a thoughtful, gifted, and analytical genius.

John Boe, a top sales trainer and speaker, has studied Hippocrates' theory extensively and uses his system of temperament styles for his sales training. According to Boe, the temperament styles are broken down as described below:

The Choleric (Worker) is:
Extroverted – Determined – Demanding – Domineering – Controlling – Practical – Self-reliant – Decisive – Independent – Confident – Goal-oriented – Risk-taker – Aggressive – Insensitive – Impatient

The Sanguine (Talker) is:
Extroverted – Enthusiastic – Emotional – Sociable – Impulsive – Articulate – Optimistic – Persuasive – Self-absorbed – Generous – Egotistical – Charming – Unorganized – Playful – Personable

The Phlegmatic (Watcher) is:
Introverted – Accommodating – Harmonious – Agreeable – Indecisive – Uninvolved – Sympathetic – Undermining – Patient – Supportive – Stable – Possessive – Passive – Selfish – Bashful – Tolerant

The Melancholy (Thinker) is:
Introverted – Analytical – Thoughtful – Organized – Critical – Shy – Detailed – Pessimistic – Sensitive – Diplomatic – Economical – Loyal – Introspective – Private – Conscientious – Moody

Carl Jung and Personality Types
In 1921, Swiss psychiatrist Carl Jung expanded on Hippocrates' theories by publishing his book *Psychological Types*. In this book, Jung proposed, based on the evidence of his years of working closely with hundreds of psychiatric patients, that people come in eight different psychological "flavors," depending on which of four mental "functions" they preferred using the most, and on whether they were "introverted" (preferring the inner, subjective world of thoughts, ideas, and emotions) or "extraverted" (preferring the outer, objective world of things, people, and actions).

The judgmental functions are ways of judging, or making decisions based on the data we take into our conscious minds from our perceptive functions. Jung called our two ways of judging "thinking" and "feeling." By thinking, Jung meant making decisions based on deductive logic. By feeling, he meant making decisions based on emotions.

Jung believed that within these two categories, there are two opposite ways of functioning. We can perceive information via 1) our senses, or 2) our intuition. We can make decisions based on 1) objective logic, or 2) subjective feelings. While we all use these four functions in our lives, each individual uses the different functions with a varying amount of success and frequency. Thus, we can identify an order of preference for these functions within individuals.

The function that someone uses most frequently is his "dominant" function. The dominant function is supported by an auxiliary (2nd) function, tertiary (3rd) function, and inferior (4th) function. Jung asserted that individuals either "extraverted" or "introverted" their dominant functions and felt that the dominant function was so important, that it overshadowed all of the other functions in terms of defining personality type. Therefore, Jung defined eight personality types:

E – Extraverted: turned toward the outer world of people and things. An extravert, or extraverted type, is one whose dominant function is focused in an external direction. Extraverts are inclined to express themselves, using their primary function, directly.

I – Introverted: turned toward the inner world of symbols, ideals, and forms. An introvert, or introverted type, is one whose dominant function is inwardly focused. Introverts are inclined to express themselves, using their primary function, indirectly, through inference and nuance.

N – iNtuition: "Unconscious perceiving." Intuition involves the recognition of patterns, the perception of the abstract; it is a visionary sense. Extraverted intuition perceives the patterns and possibilities of life. Introverted intuition compares the "rightness" of real-world circumstances with that which is ideal. In

Jung's typology, intuition is an irrational function. Intuition's opposite function is Sensing.

S – Sensing: physiological perception; perceiving with the five natural senses. Extraverted sensors are attuned to the world of sights, sounds, smells, touches, and tastes. Introverted sensors are most aware of how those perceptions compare with their ideal internal standards. In Jung's typology, sensing is an irrational function. Sensing's opposite is iNtuition.

T – Thinking: Making decisions impersonally. In Jung's typology, thinking is a rational function. Thinking's opposite is Feeling.

F – Feeling: Making decisions from a personal perspective. In Jung's typology, feeling is a rational function. Feeling's opposite is Thinking.

P – Perceiving: *P* means that the dominant function is a Perceiving function (iNtuition or Sensing);

J – Judging: *J* means the dominant function is a deciding or Judging function.

In total, there are 16 types, consisting of four-letter combinations representing something basic about one's psychological type.

1. Extraverted Sensing (modern types: ESFP, ESTP)
2. Introverted Sensing (modern types: ISTJ, ISFJ)
3. Extraverted Intuition (modern types: ENFP, ENTP)
4. Introverted Intuition (modern types: INFJ, INTJ)
5. Extraverted Thinking (modern types: ESTJ, ENTJ)
6. Introverted Thinking (modern types: ISTP, INTP)
7. Extraverted Feeling (modern types: ESFJ, ENFJ)
8. Introverted Feeling (modern types: INFP, ISFP)

Myers-Briggs Expands on Jung's Theories
In the 1950s, a mother/daughter team known as Myers-Briggs expanded on Jung's theories. Katharine Cook Briggs (1875-1968) graduated from what later became the University of Michigan and, in 1917, constructed a personality model based on her own research. However, after reading Jung's book *Psychological Types* in 1923, she considered his model to be superior.

Daughter Isabel Briggs (now using the surname Myers as a result of her marriage to Clarence Myers), also studied and tested Jung's theories. The U.S. entry into World War II in late 1941 motivated Isabel Myers to develop a personality instrument to help people get a better fit between themselves and their jobs. To develop this instrument, Isabel constructed questions for testing against a criterion group of about 20 family and friends whose type preferences seemed clear to Katharine and Isabel.

In the late 1940s, Myers-Briggs made an agreement with Donald Mackinnon, founder of the Institute of Personality Research (ISPR) at the University of California at Berkeley to use their assessment tool, and it swiftly gained notoriety.

The DISC Method of the 1970s
Sales trainers of the 1970s recognized the value of the Myers-Briggs method for the ability to get a quick bead on their customers. Yet, as you can already anticipate, the testing process is technical and laborious, and the various combinations of letters could get confusing.

Thus the DISC method of personality typing was born. The anagram "DISC" represents:

"**D**" - Dominant/Driver or Fast-Paced and Task-Oriented
"**I**" - Influencing/Inspiring or Fast-Paced and People-Oriented
"**S**" - Stable/Steady or Slower-Paced and People-Oriented
"**C**" - Compliant/Correct or Slower-Paced and Task-Oriented

The DISC method was successful in helping sales professionals and others in business who need quick, simple insight into their clients and customers.

Today, professional speakers and sales trainers have used the DISC method as the basis for developing their own personality-type systems. Some people use colors to represent the four different personality types, whereas others might use shapes.

Introducing the More-Personality System for Writers

After studying the Enneagram, Jung, and Myers-Briggs, I worked them into a system. Screenwriters found that my system enabled them to get an immediate grasp on their characters, and enabled them to flesh out their characters, given each personality type's needs, fears, and desires.

Brief Descriptions of the More-Personality System

Below are the four styles of the More-Personality system. I will expand on this at length later in this chapter, but you will find the descriptions useful for the quiz to come.

Mover – brash, "Type A" personality, result driven, fast moving & thinking;
Observer – factual, observant, often insecure, focused on detail, aloof;
Relater – encourages & motivates others, service-oriented, likes human contact;
Energizer – storyteller, confident, ambitious, likeable, charming, quick thinking;

The More-Personality Style Quiz

To find out your characters' personality styles, slip into their bodies and answer the questions as your characters would answer. In the More-Personality system, a *style* is a way a character naturally acts in a typical situation.

Before you have your character take the personality quiz, you may wish to see an example of how a character – specifically, Vivian as played by Julia Roberts in the film *Pretty Woman* – would take the quiz. You will find her worksheet and answers in the Appendix.

Instructions:

Step One
In each of the five boxes below, examine the four descriptive adjectives as they may – or may not – describe you (or your character).

1. For each line, rank the adjective that most nearly describes your character as the "7."
2. The next closest, mark as the "5."
3. The next closest, mark the "3."
4. The word that least closely describes you, mark as "1."

Each box should have four adjectives ranked 7, 5, 3, and 1.
1.   __ A. Obstinate
     __ B. Beguiling
     __ C. Genial
     __ D. Docile

2.   __ A. Aggressive
     __ B. Fun-loving
     __ C. Agreeable
     __ D. Compliant

3. __ A. Courageous
    __ B. Ability to Dazzle
    __ C. Balanced
    __ D. Exact

4. __ A. Resolute
    __ B. Scheming
    __ C. Amiable
    __ D. Guarded

5. __ A. Demanding
    __ B. Cheerful
    __ C. Easy-going
    __ D. Scrupulous

Step Two

Transfer your numerical responses to this answer sheet and then total columns A, B, C, D

	A	B	C	D
1.				
2.				
3.				
4.				
5.				
Total				

Step Three
Now it's time to transfer your scores to the following boxes

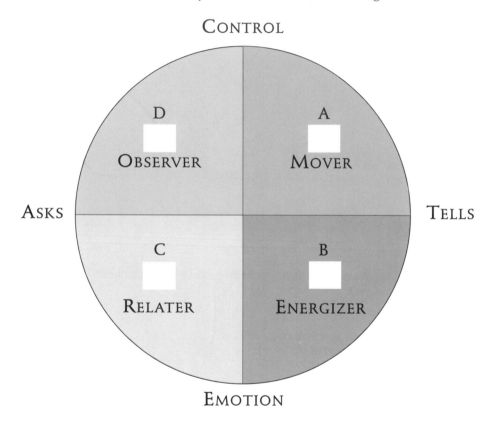

Fill in your score here

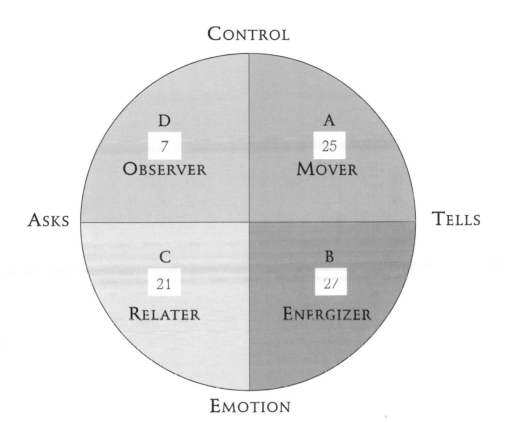

How Julia Robert's Vivian Pretty Woman *would score*

Before you analyze your own score (or that of your character) please turn your attention to the box marked "How Julia Robert's Vivian (*Pretty Woman*) would score." (Reminder: Her quiz worksheet can be found in the Appendix.)

As you can see, Vivian scored highest in the A and B quadrants. This is her "natural personality style."

Before we go further, let's take a closer look at what the types represented by the quadrants mean.

The quadrant "B" represents the personality style I call the Energizer. The second highest score can be found in the "A" quadrant, which represents a style I call the Mover. Vivian scored lowest in the quadrants "C" and "D," which belong to the styles I call the Observer and the Relater.

Understanding the Styles
One-line descriptions of the four basic styles of the More-Personality system are listed below. Rely on your first instinct to quickly assign a "type" to your main and other characters.

Then, once you've assigned a style to your character, read the detailed section on that character with a notebook (or open computer file) at the ready. Consider each of the statements and questions that pertain to your character's natural style, and be prepared to answer the question or brainstorm exciting plot ideas in your notebook.

Also, be aware of the potential to create additional characters to play up or showcase your character's natural style. These can be casual "information passer" type characters, or significant relationships, both in terms of your character's growth and development, as well as plot.

You will learn volumes of information about your characters in this exercise, so you are strongly encouraged to prepare yourself for taking down the information in your notebook as soon as you arrive at this section.

Once Again, Quick Descriptions of the More-Personality System

Mover – brash, "Type A" personality, result driven, fast moving & thinking;

Observer – factual, observant, often insecure, focused on detail, aloof;

Relater – encourages & motivates others, service-oriented, likes human contact.

Energizer – storyteller, confident, ambitious, likeable, charming, quick thinking;

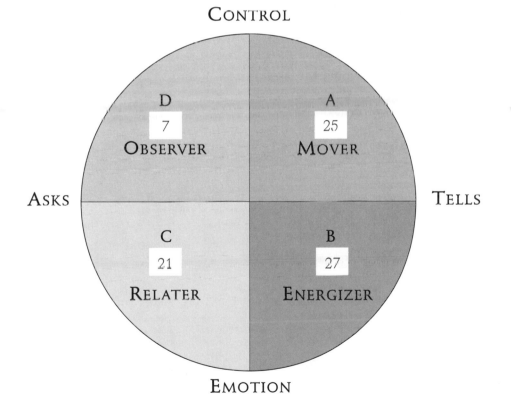

More-Personality Chart

Many real-life individuals and characters are combinations of the two types. In our earlier example, Vivian was primarily an Energizer, but her score revealed she was also very close to a Mover.

In this scenario, you would read the Energizer style, and later, if you need to add more complexity or need a new bead on your character, read the Mover section.

The Energizer

The world of film and literature is rich in characters with the Energizer personality. Often, Energizers are the main characters of the story or film because they are exciting, attractive, and energetically in quest of a goal. More passive personality styles are drawn to them in fascination and because they secretly wish to have their energy, drive, and passion.

Scarlett O'Hara, played by Vivian Leigh in the film *Gone with the Wind*, is a good example of an Energizer. So was the role played by Tom Cruise in *Jerry Maguire*. Real-life examples of the Energizer style include a fair amount of actors, as well as individuals who've achieved fame for their abilities and are noted for their engaging charm. This group includes athletes O. J. Simpson and Kobe Bryant, who have faced violent criminal charges, yet retain a core fan base.

The supposition that charm goes a long way in helping the Energizer personality style along in life is an important one to consider. This style can be used to build the kind of character who manipulates his way through life, trading on a heady combination of intelligence, wit, inherent likeability, natural ability, and instinctively knowing how best to play the hand he's been dealt.

Both luck and hard work are responsible for the Energizer's success in life. Of all the styles, the Energizer is the most likeable because he operates with a "win-win" mentality and feels a responsibility to dazzle and charm on command.

Energizers often have a smile, good word, and quick joke for everyone, but are often quite different in their private lives. If your character is an Energizer, you are well advised to consider that your character may have two distinct sides to his personality. For example, an Energizer is always "on" – whether trying to charm colleagues or his kids at home. Yet radiating all that energy is draining. Try to place them in scenes where you capture their reflective nature to give the character (and the audience) a break from all that excitement.

As a general rule, Energizers do not have other Energizers as friends or lovers. Such a relationship is competitive by its nature, as Energizers have a deep-rooted need to be the star. One can speculate that the reason the Tom Cruise/Nicole Kidman marriage didn't work out was because they were both Energizers.

Female Energizers are drawn to male Movers or high-powered Observers, while male Energizers are drawn toward any of the remaining personality styles. While it's possible for a female Energizer to build a relationship with a male Relater, her main objective is power and status. She needs a mate who can help fuel and accomplish her dreams.

Below are traits of the Energizer style combined with exercises designed to stimulate your creative mind. Again, try to answer them with your notebook or computer file open and ready and your imagination in high gear.

1. Your Energizer has been called "extroverted, lively, and vivacious" at various times in his life. Jot down scenes from his life when he heard these remarks. Also, ask yourself: does your character really believe he is lively and vivacious, or would he

say this is an act he puts on to charm people and get what he wants.

2. Your Energizer is keenly aware of trends and dresses as well as he can afford. He's unable to deny himself anything that will improve his looks or status. Ask yourself: Do you think your Energizer would ever resort to crime to get what he wants? Shoplifting?

3. Energizers are often spontaneous and uninhibited, but there is a method to their madness. Energizers also have varying tolerances for risk. Can you see your Energizer ever getting so drunk or high he risks looking the fool? If you can see it happen, when and why would it happen?

4. Energizers are storytellers. They love hearing stories, are suckers for a good yarn, are swept to emotion and acts of kindness with a good story (witness Bette Davis in the opening scene of *All About Eve* getting teary eyed and moved to action by the self-deprecating Eve's hard luck story).

Bette Davis, as the actress Margo Channing, listens to Eve tell her sob story

Consider scenes in which you can have your Energizer tell an engaging story to charm an individual or group. Consider constructing a scene in which you can move your Energizer to action by hearing another character tell a good story.

5. Your Energizer is flamboyant. Consider his wardrobe. While an Energizer likes designer clothes and being in fashion, he resents looking like everyone else and appreciates a unique touch. Look at your Energizer and ask how you can skew his appearance to visually dramatize his flamboyant nature.

6. Your Energizer is compulsively addicted to new goals, new friends, new activities, new places, and fun. Boredom is an anxiety-provoking fear. What does your character do in "boring situations" such as waiting at the airport or the doctor's office?

7. Most Energizers are excessive personalities. In a worst-case scenario, they are greedy, demanding, and self-centered. How has this affected their relationships in the past? How does it affect their current relationships?

8. Many Energizers are easily addicted to alcohol, drugs, food, gambling, and more because they are "stimulation junkies" and always need a project on the fire. Substance abuse can temporarily hide the pain of waiting/watching/hoping for the dream to materialize. Does your Energizer have an addiction? What is it? Why and how did it develop?

9. One reason Energizers can be so easily addicted and feel compelled to be the life of the party is that they fought for attention as children and never felt as if they "had enough." Is this true of your character? What was his relationship with his parents like?

10. While nine out of 10 people find the Energizer charming, one person out of that 10 will find him rude or arrogant. Among

your Energizer's circle of admirers, is there one character who dislikes him? Who and why?

11.   Many Energizers have erratic mood swings. One reason is that they are always striving, and are frustrated when they encounter opposition. Can you think of scenes which would motivate a mood swing?

12.   The compulsive, spontaneous nature of an Energizer can form the basis for great scenes that would rival the famous scene in the film *La Dolce Vita* when the characters jumped into the Trevi Fountain. What impulsive actions can you see your character take that would develop his personality, as well as further the story?

13.   Energizers have many acquaintances but few genuine friends. Still, they are considered "centers of influence" by all who know them. People ask their recommendations on cool, fun restaurants, clubs, and travel destinations. Consider writing a list of your Energizer's favorite places, and the kind of people who would seek out his opinion.

14.   Energizers are expert "multi-taskers" and like to pack many experiences in a single activity. They are rarely "in the moment." As a result, they are not as focused as they should be. Consider scenes in which this can pose problems for them, either in their work or personal relationships.

15.   Appearance is very important to Energizers, as they trade on their charm. Consider your character's appearance. If he had to choose, what would he splurge on? Shoes? A suit? Is he overly occupied with his hair? Is there something he wants to change in himself?

16. If forced to chose between being too flashy and conservative, Energizers often err on the side of being flashy. They like to be noticed. Erin Brockovich (the person and the character played by Julia Roberts in the film of the same name) was an Energizer whose flashy wardrobe – inappropriate for her work – revealed much about her character. Consider ways you can use clothing to showcase character.

17. Energizers can also become addicted to people, such as coaches or mentors. They easily become dependent on whoever eases their anxiety or gives them pleasure. Who would this person be in your story?

18. At their lowest point, Energizers stand in danger of becoming manic-depressive. Do you see this trait in your character?

19. Energizers fear failure and humiliation, and try to project their image to make a favorable impression, even if they have to misrepresent themselves or distort their accomplishments. Is this true of your Energizer? Can you list his fears, and ways they may distort his accomplishments?

20. Though Energizers try and usually do make good impressions, at low points, they may resort to arrogant, snide behavior and sarcastic retorts. Can you see your Energizer doing this? Where would he do this in your story?

21. Energizers crave fame. They love the limelight and believe their own press. In your story, how could their narcissist behavior be their blessing, as well as their curse?

22. An energizer can be both the hero of a story, as well as its villain. Look at your Energizer, and decide how he can go either way.

The Mover

Seen in his best light, the Mover personality makes the world go around. Like the Energizer, he is often the main character of the story or film because of his drive and ability to focus on the bottom line.

Unlike Energizers, Movers (even good looking Movers) do not trade on charm. They have a "big picture" mentality and are quick to deal with anyone who steps between themselves and their objectives. Movers enjoy using their wits to meet the challenges of the outside world, and also look forward to adversity because the challenge invigorates them and makes them stronger.

Humphrey Bogart, both the actor and the character style he often played, characterizes the Mover type in that he keenly observed situations before opening his mouth or taking an action. Other Mover styles included actor Sylvester Stallone, Frank Sinatra (as well as many of the characters he played) and characters portrayed by Kathleen Turner (especially *Body Heat*) and Sharon Stone (*Basic Instinct*).

Nothing stops a Mover from achieving his goals

Female Movers often can be confused with Energizers since charm, seduction, and beauty are often the tools of their trade. In most cases, they are an equal mix of both Energizer and Mover. The deciding factor in giving them the Mover category is:

- ✓ Inner strength and resources;
- ✓ Ability to focus and concentrate;
- ✓ Aura of power and control;
- ✓ Curt, ruthless personality and intolerance of time-wasters.

The Mover protagonist is admired by those who know him, seeing him as a stern but benevolent taskmaster. Movers work hard for their seats of power and pride themselves on their accomplishments. Unlike the Energizer, the Mover does not believe in the concept of "Fake it until you make it" or spinning a career with smoke and mirrors.

In real and reel life, Movers are usually not immediately likeable. They don't try to charm or take pains to be pleasant. In fact, their blunt manner can put many people off. Yet when they are at their best, Movers are natural leaders to whom everyone looks in a time of crisis. They can be excellent but stern mentors and can go out of their way to help others climb the ladder of success.

Movers crave control and power above all else. Unlike Energizers, they have the focus and patience to methodically plot their course and can wait years, even decades, for their plan to come to fruition.

Keenly observant of the world around them, Movers take nothing at face value. Credibility is essential to the Mover, and everyone in his social or business circle must prove his worth.

Male Movers can be overbearing in personal relationships, as their desire to prove their superiority takes place both in the office and private residence. Their "macho" behavior can be problematic in marriages, and their desire to "conquer" can take form in adulterous affairs. The women who do earn a Male Mover's respect think like they do, and are Movers themselves.

The traits and exercises listed below may stimulate your creative thinking about your Mover character.

1. Movers fear being controlled by others. How can you give this fear form in your work?

2. In both fiction and film, it's important to "show rather than tell" a character's personality. Can you think of ways to show your Mover's willpower, confidence, and challenging personality through specific scenes?

3. A stellar characteristic of a Mover is his ability to turn a set-back into a new opportunity. Can this element work in your story?

4. Movers are surprisingly intuitive and work on hunches. Is there a place to work this into your story?

5. Shrewd observers of the outside world, Movers often see gold where others see dust. This ability makes for effective financial managers and real estate developers. What is your Mover's profession and how is his Mover style responsible for his success?

6. Movers can spot an individual with potential (but low self esteem) and build him up until he is useful. Can you see a scenario such as this taking place in your story?

7. Movers often fear they will be unable to accomplish their mission. What is your Mover's mission, and what are some obstacles that can threaten it? How can you showcase the "iron man's" fears in your story?

8. While Movers can give praise where praise is do, they are quick to criticize. They are also pathologically territorial. Altercations usually arise when someone threatens their territory. Can you see such an altercation in your story? Whom would your Mover be struggling against?

9. Movers often "move into" a situation. When they see a void, or an opportunity, they are quick to fill it. Have you seen evidence of this in your Mover's life?

10. Female Movers are often categorized as pushy. If your Mover is female, what do others say about her behind her back? How does she feel about it?

11. Movers are often resented. In your story, who resents your Mover and why?

12. Movers pride themselves on their intelligence, and can as easily be found among U.S. presidents, as well as the most ruthless of criminals. Qualities that unite all Movers are faith in themselves to achieve their desires, and a compelling need to show power and quickly turn ideas into action. Are there other elements that are driving your Mover?

13. As criminals, Movers are energized by each successful heist. Nothing detours them, aside from death or arrest. A criminal Mover will never muse if it's time to "get out of the business." If your Mover is a criminal, consider that progressive scenes should strengthen and fuel his resolve.

14. Movers can work as secondary characters, but realize that they can easily take center stage. Actor/producer Gregory Peck knew this when he asked actor Robert Mitchum to play the villain, Max Cady, against his own role as the mild-mannered protagonist, Sam Bowden in the 1962 version of *Cape Fear*. As an actor, Peck knew Mitchum's personality and strong, dominating Mover role would turn him into the lead character. As producer, he was willing to let go of his ego.

You may find yourself having to rebuild your story in the second act when your Mover character begins getting territorial.

15. Movers live in worlds of their own. They are commanders who may experience delusions of grandeur, which, historically, is responsible for both their successes and failures. Is there a moment in your story where you can give the audience a touch of your Mover's noble goal?

The Observer
In the world of literature, Sherlock Holmes, Miss Maples, and Detective Poirot share the Observer personality style. The hallmark of Observers is that they observe everything with extraordinary perceptiveness and insight, even if they don't "seem the type" – such as Lt. Columbo played by Peter Falk in the TV series *Columbo*.

In real life, this group includes virtually every profession, yet its members are characterized by their analytical nature. In contrast to the Energizer, this personality style demands verification of all information. Before giving a talk, an Observer reads volumes of information and is careful to backup all sources.

As a group, they are highly independent and focused, often to the extent that they live in their own worlds. They are wary of strangers and new information until credibility can be established. When President Reagan spoke of a new alliance with the Russians, he used the words: "Trust, but verify."

This is the credo of the Observer.

Well-educated Observers take pride in their keen intelligence and excel in occupations involving law, science, mathematics, architects, and of course, as detectives.

Observers usually play out scenarios in their minds before taking actions. Their worst fear is to be "proven" wrong or stand corrected. Being correct is paramount to them, and they will go to irrational lengths to prove it.

Observers function at many different levels. At their best, they are top notch scientists or attorneys, well versed in every aspect, every minute detail, of their professions. Many Observers can be found on Court TV, where as attorneys, they find the most obscure details of the law that get their clients out of jail, free. Most detectives are Observers, as they take pleasure in analyzing and piecing together the elements of crime.

Albert Einstein was an Observer, as are Stephen King and director David Lynch.

Each of the four basic personality styles of the More-Personality system has its share of polar opposites, namely people who range from high-functioning top executives to raving lunatics. Yet as a whole, the wall between genius and insanity is thinnest with the Observer type.

Reasons for this include the Observers' intense desire to always be right, and their terror of being wrong or unable to convince others of their keen, superior intelligence. Anxious by nature, many Observers lose it completely when a world they've defined by their own logic suddenly seems illogical – and there's nothing they can do about it.

Below are traits of the Observer style and exercises to stimulate your creative mind. Again, try to answer them with your note-book or computer file open and ready.

1. Observers observe everything with vivid sensual perception. In the adaptation of the classic novel *The Forsyte Saga*, the character Soames Forsyte sniffs his wife's freshly laundered lingerie once he's found she left him.

This visceral image conveys a great deal of information about the Observer's keen power of perception. As Observers enter a room, their eyes dart about, gathering information as they sniff to uncover yet more detail. Mentally, they also are accessing the people in the room, using their attire to categorize them and dis-cover "what kind of people they may be."

Imagine your Observer character entering a new room and situ-ation for the first time. How does he look at the other characters in the scene? What does he notice?

2. It's said that curiosity killed the cat. Can you think of a situa-tion in your story where being too curious got your Observer in trouble (or, instigated the action)?

3. Like a cat, an Observer is independent and aloof. How does this shade his personal relationships?

4. Unlike Energizers who are easily distracted, an Observer can be so involved in a project he fails to notice the time pass. Is this a characteristic of your Observer? How will you use it?

5. Both Energizers and Movers tend to rush into projects, fueled by a heady combination of confidence and enthusiasm. The very thought of rushing into any activity without the proper research is anathema to an Observer, who has a morbid fear of failure and ridicule.

Observers work things out in their minds to their satisfaction before bringing their ideas out. Is there evidence of this tendency in your character? How does it manifest itself?

6. An Observer's ability to observe the world in detail keeps him sane. When he turns his attention to focusing on his interpretations of the world, he can lose touch with reality. Can you visualize a scene in which this may happen to your Observer character?

7. Observers are easily fascinated by esoteric subjects. The old stereotype of a computer geek (long hair, unwashed clothing, preoccupied with technology) is an example of what can happen to Observers when they lose themselves in a project. The story of scientist John Nash in *A Beautiful Mind* (2001), is a deeper, darker example of how the Observer can descend into madness.

John Nash, lost in the world of scientific theories

Is your Observer reaching the point of mental illness in his quest to prove his theory?

8. One of the negative traits of the Observer includes the propensity to belittle others. Sometimes this happens as a defense mechanism to prove their mental superiority over an inferior, other times it's a way of keeping the social world at bay so they can be left alone to complete their projects.

Does your Observer belittle people? Why? What has he to gain?

9. Some Observers maintain a social life, but the majority neither seeks out a wide variety of friends nor finds value in them. Many Observers find that spending time with others detracts from time they can spend with their projects.

Observers are also tough friends to keep, as their insistence on proving they are right often drives others away.

What is the shape of your Observer's social life? What do his friends think of him? Despite his smug airs, why do they keep him as a friend?

10. Observers act and react out of the conviction that the only things they can believe in are themselves, their concepts, their version of reality, and their own observations. How does this manifest itself in your character?

11. If an Energizer enjoys money for the status it can buy in terms of clothes, trendy restaurants, and luxury resorts, an Observer hordes money. What is he saving for? If he did spend money, what would he use it for?

12. Some Observers do have social ambitions, yet they are reluctant to throw themselves into society until they've "made it." The term means different things to different Observers. Some, such as a Bill Gates wannabe (Gates is an Observer type) may feel he has to put together the perfect computer software. Others may feel they must make a certain amount of money.

What does your Observer feel is a sure, verifiable sign of success and how will he know when he's made it?

13. If an Observer does have friends, his friends don't know all that much about him. Some might know him because of a sport, such as bowling, but know little more about his life. Another friend might be a work buddy. The Observer reveals very little of himself in conversation.

Does your Observer meet someone in the course of your story? Why does the Observer let this person into his life? How much does he reveal of himself?

14. Observers – regardless if they show it or not – are usually high strung and nervous. Their metabolism usually runs at a high pitch. Some Observers look emaciated, almost as if nerves, anxiety, and pressure are eating away at their flesh.

How would you describe the ways anxiety and pressure impact your Observer's appearance?

15. Relationships are difficult for the Observer. Skeptical and suspicious by nature, he often feels as if everything must have a catch.

Is your Observer in a relationship? What keeps it together? What does he crave in a relationship?

16. One negative characteristic of the Observer is that he may show off his knowledge to smugly establish superiority over others, or as a way of injecting a negative tone in a conversation.

Is your Observer a show-off? If so, why? If not, why not?

17. Another negative trait of the Observer is that he is antagonistic to people he considers a threat to his world. For example, if a married Observer is jealous of a "family friend" who is monopolizing his spouse's attention, he might make an underhanded, snide remark under his breath.

Can you see a situation in which your Observer would be antagonistic? Why? To whom?

18. In their often unconscious quest for complete self-sufficiency, Observers sometimes keep people out of their lives. They may say they yearn for companionship but once they meet people, will drive them away.

Does your Observer do this? If so, can you see him change? What would instigate this change?

The Relater

In an office environment, the Relater can usually be found in the Human Resources department. Unlike the Mover personality style – who demands "just the bullet points" of whatever you are going to say, the Relater wants you to sit down first, make yourself at home, have some tea, and nibble on a cookie. As you may suspect, the Relater is a "people person."

This personality style enjoys being helpful and of service to everyone he or she meets, even strangers. They also like to be in agreement with others, and will go out of their way to go with the flow rather than insist on their own agenda. In old James Bond films, a perfect Relater would be the secretary, Miss Moneypenny, to James Bond.

Relaters are always looking out for the welfare of others, particularly if they are secretaries, wives, or mothers to the other parties. They like to talk and gossip, and tend to touch people a lot.

People pleasers, they often resort to flattery to motivate other people to like them and want them around. Relaters set out to make themselves needed, so that other people will always want them around.

As mothers, they often suffocate in their desire to impose their love on their offspring, though their real desire is to be loved in return. Because they give so freely, they expect love in return, and often are devastated when it is not reciprocated.

In a family environment, Relaters position themselves to be at the center of things. They are the ones who keep in touch with distant family members and check in with closer relatives often to see what's up and how they can be of service. In return, they expect to be viewed as the cement that holds the family together.

A good fictional example of a Relater character is the female impersonator/mother played by Nathan Lane, co-starring with Robin Williams in *The Birdcage* (1996). Though a bit over the top, Lane's drag queen character "Mrs. 'Mother' Coleman" dramatized the lengths a Relater would go to "sacrifice" oneself and prove loyalty to the family.

Nathan Lane in drag playing "Mrs. Coleman" and
embracing her new daughter-in-law

Relaters hold a similar position in an office environment, where they are the "go-to" person for all the latest gossip. They are nosey, asking the most personal of questions and violating personal space, sitting close to strangers, and taking liberties of friendship.

Below are traits of the Relater style and exercises to stimulate your creative thinking. Note that it will be difficult to make a Relater your protagonist, mostly because the very idea of rocking the boat is abhorrent to them. Though they enjoy gossip, they would be devastated to hear that their loose tongues resulted in people losing their jobs or some other tragedies. Stories are all about dramatic conflict. By their very nature, Relaters seek to avoid discord whenever possible.

1. Relaters have a tendency to get overly friendly with people very quickly. How can you use this information to create a scene that would generate a conflict or plot complication in your story?

2. Relaters have a "secret agenda." They want everyone to recognize them and give them their due, yet at the same time, they feel uncomfortable asking for this attention outright. Their mindset is that "if I do nice things for people and am always of service, everyone will love me." Unrequited love and lack of respect (when they feel such respect is deserved) can throw a Relater into a tailspin.

Consider the Relater in your story. Can you create a list of things that would set them off? It could form the basis of a very comedic scene.

3. Each of the four personality styles in the More-Personality system has a unique way of speaking. The Mover tends to be upfront and ask questions in a brusque manner. The Energizer is an expert at conveying information that highlights his own charm and wit. The Observer asks pointed questions, and can sometimes seem as if he's cross examining, not conversing.

Yet Relaters can speak in one of two voices. One voice is the flatterer, often used upon the initial meeting. The second voice is that of the nagging mother or jilted spouse, meant to instill guilt when they feel their personal needs are not meant.

Consider your Relaters. Do they always speak in the same tone? Or do they let frustration give a certain shrillness to their voice?

4.   All Relaters seek to be indispensable and impossible to replace. In the scheme of your story, how does the Relater accomplish this?

5.   Relaters usually work in "helping" professions or as assistants, office managers, and human resource executives. What does your Relater do and how does it fit in with your story?

6.   Secretly, Relaters are highly dependant on having others notice and acknowledge them, yet their fear is that this dependence will show. How does this play out with your Relater character?

7.   As individuals, some Relaters like associating with the rich and powerful, others like making themselves indispensable to the needy and psychologically or physically damaged. How does your Relater see himself?

8.   Relaters act as the archetypes of good parents, always looking out for the welfare of their charges and empowering them to grow and discover their strengths. For whom does your Relater look out in your story?

9.   Most Relaters are religious, if only for the ritual of going to their places of worship and being seen in worship by others. This reinforces their need to be seen as helpful members of their community. How does this desire manifest itself in your Relater character?

10. Some Relaters like to be thought of as saviors and miracle workers. They may adopt children or become active in Big Sister/Big Brother programs. If your Relater is single, how does he "share the love" or volunteer for a cause?

11. A few Relater types are psychologically imbalanced in that they set out to seduce a group of people, make them dependent, and then lord over them. Can you see your Relater indulging in such behavior?

12. Relaters believe in "giving before they get." Once your Relater exhausts himself giving of his time, energy, and resources, he expects positive feedback. If this feedback isn't instantly forthcoming, he may prod for it, or secretly complain to others. Would your Relater follow this model?

13. At their lowest point, Relaters can be accused of being interfering. An example of this is the mother figure in the TV show *Everybody Loves Raymond*. Would your Relater turn into a vocal nag, or is he the type who would instead complain to others?

14. One effective way to use a Relater in your story is to make him a character who gives unasked for advice. The advice might be the so-called rational thing to do, but the audience is rooting for the central character to follow his gut feeling. Is there a way you can use a Relater in this capacity?

15. Some Relaters are busybodies, and act as "information carriers" in that they bring gossip to the forefront. Can you find a way to use a Relater like this?

16. In their quest to be popular and the center of information, many Relaters resort to shameless gossip and talk about others in embarrassingly explicit detail. Is there a way to create and use a Relater character in your story to reveal colorful backstory on another character?

17. In the film *All About Eve* (1950), the character of Eve (played by Anne Baxter) pretended to be a Relater and insinuated herself in the life of Margo Channing (Bette Davis) by becoming a combination secretary/maid/psychiatrist. In actuality, Eve was a master manipulator and a Mover.

Can you see any one of your characters "pretending" to be a Relater to get the upper hand?

18. Many Relaters feel they have proprietary dibs on their friends, and are anxious and jealous if friends get together without them.

If you have a Relater in your story, how does he feel about friends getting together without him? Can you think of some plot-advancing scenes in which you can use this powerful emotion?

19. At their worst, Relaters can be seen as smothering to give attention and receive attention, in return. Taken to an extreme, their frustration may motivate them to belittle others "the name of love." Can you use this trait in your story?

◆ CHAPTER SUMMARY ◆

In this chapter you learned:

1. Human beings are "pre-wired" to identify strangers according to "types" of that style they have met in the past.

2. Personality style type-casting has a long, ancient, and scholarly history.

3. The More-Personality system is a powerful tool to help you learn more about your characters and their relationships.

4. Enabling each character to take the More-Personality system quiz will allow you to learn more about each of their individual styles, and if necessary, give characters new styles to further conflict in your story.

5. By categorizing each character into a type, and mastering the traits of that type, you are able to produce more believable characters.

◆ ASSIGNMENTS ◆

1. If you currently are working on a story, give each character one of the four styles.

2. On 3 x 5 index cards (preferably colored) write the name of the character and his character style on the unlined side. On the lined side, list both traits and answers to the questions posed in this chapter.

3. With your cards in hand and your notebook or computer file open, explore whether all the character styles work together in the kind of symbiotic relationship that would allow for maximum conflict and the progression of the plot. If not, consider giving difficult characters the traits of another style.

◆ CHAPTER TWO ◆

MAXIMIZING CONFLICT THROUGH PERSONALITY TYPES

All successful screenplays and novels are about relationships between characters. As you discovered in the last chapter, what makes stories interesting is discovering the complexity within characters, and waiting with anticipation for the fireworks that have been building between characters via plot conflict and personality style to begin.

In this chapter, we will revisit classic films to take apart and analyze character dynamics via personality styles as described using the More-Personality system. We will explore why natural conflicts arise when various personality styles meet and clash, and also investigate the inherent qualities that motivate one character to fall in love with another.

Let's start with the film *Chinatown* (1974), starring Jack Nicholson and Faye Dunaway. To recap the plot, a private investigator in L.A. (Nicholson) during the 1930s becomes accidentally caught up in a plot revolving around water rights, corrupt politicians, millionaires, and a woman (Dunaway) protecting her daughter by an incestuous relationship with her corrupt millionaire father.

Nicholson, like most heroic figures, is a Mover. He makes things happen.

Now before I tell you, guess the personality style of Dunaway's character, Evelyn Cross Mulwray?

Chances are, you replied "Energizer" because as you can imagine, even if you haven't seen the film, she is beautiful, seductive, and the leading lady. Yet in the previous chapter, we established that the Energizer style is primarily preoccupied with "self." Their driving goal is to see their glorious reflection in the eyes of others and acquire all the accoutrements of fame.

In the scheme of things, Dunaway's character of Evelyn Cross Mulwray is actually a "Relater" in that her total focus and concern is on protecting her daughter/sister.

Key to Understanding Types

Whenever you need to figure out if a character is a Mover or an Energizer, a Relater or Observer, ask yourself this definitive question:

What is his or her ultimate objective?

Jake Gittes (played by Nicholson) was a Mover character in that he enjoyed overcoming obstacles. He welcomed challenges. He saw himself as the hero and could not even envision losing. Fame did not matter to him in the way it would be crucial to an Energizer. Gittes was focused on solving the mystery, even if he died trying.

Yes, Eveyln Mulwray was as seductive as an Energizer and as powerful as a Mover. Yet she only used seduction and power as a means to her personal end, which was to ensure her daughter's safety. A traditional Energizer would care only for herself and her own social success or creature comforts.

Fictional Relationships

In films and novels, the longest-lasting man/woman relationship is that of the Mover/Relater. Quite often, it is a satisfying marriage of convenience. In the Michael Douglas feature film *Fatal Attraction* (1987), Douglas' character was a Mover with strong Energizer qualities who married a housewife Relater, happy to spend her life taking care of Douglas, the kid, and the dog. Their happy marriage was threatened by Douglas' affair with the sultry Energizer character played by Glenn Close.

Mover/Energizer relationships (and Energizer/Energizer relationships) are characterized by incredible passion that often leads to violence. In real life, one can look to the murder/suicide of *Saturday Night Live* comedian Phil Hartman and his wife Brynn. Phil Hartman was a successful Mover/Energizer in that he found fame in his chosen field. Brynn, an Energizer who craved fame, was forced by circumstance and society into the role of the "Relater" – a wife, mother, and helpmate to the "real" star in the home.

The Mover/Energizer and Energizer/Energizer competitive pairing is fraught with conflict, high emotion, and never-ending drama. Film stars who marry within their field often divorce. Elizabeth Taylor, with her many marriages, is a perfect example.

Even though male Energizers and Movers "need" Relaters to look after them, sexually and emotionally, they crave the fiery seductress who already has mesmerized the public and proves a formidable challenge. Yet once she is conquered, once she loses her attraction to the masses and unwittingly turns into a wife and mother (now conquered and his possession) the male Energizer/Mover loses interest.

Female Energizers/Movers face a tougher road. They are attracted to powerful men and count on their ability to master them, but too often, the tables turn and their mates have the upper hand. For female Movers, it means they remain single until quite late in life. For female Energizers, they will stay in the relationship as long as the man retains his status, power, and can be useful to her.

Female Relaters

If you are tempted to put a female Relater in your story, ask yourself if she is a "true" Relater or if, like the Eve character in *All About Eve*, she is just pretending – either as part of her nefarious strategy or because this type of persona is most readily accepted by society.

In the 1980s, National Public Radio once surveyed typical Americans regarding their thoughts about First Lady, the senior Mrs. Bush. One male commenter remarked that he approved of Mrs. Bush because "she looks like a wife and mother."

Pressure to embody a specific societal ideal is strongest the further one moves away from large, cosmopolitan cities and the closer one identifies with solid family and religious values.

As you sketch out your story, be certain to investigate your character's backstory, as it will have a huge impact on his present life.

In the years before the 1960s, many women fashioned themselves into Relaters, whether they felt like playing the supporting role in their families or not. Curiously, in the 80s and 90s, women who were not natural Movers took on this role, seeking out advanced professional degrees and working full time well into marriage and motherhood.

So as you create your characters, try to figure out if societal trends may be driving them into roles that are not their desire by nature.

Understanding the Psyche of Your Character

To understand your characters well, you must discover their greatest fears and threaten them at every appropriate opportunity.

In the film *Wall Street* (1987), Michael Douglas played a Mover – a financial genius who plotted and manipulated his way to success. Failure was his worst fear, and to avoid it he was driven to crime.

John Malkovich played another Mover type as the Vicomte de Valmont in the film *Dangerous Liaisons* (1988). Money and business success were not the objectives for Valmont, winning a bet was – even (or especially) if it involved betrayal and murder. For Mover personalities, the more challenges thrown their way, the better. Nothing short of death will stop them from achieving their goals once they determine they are in the game.

Observers have a strong constitution, but can not match the strength of Movers. At the top of their game, Observers are rational and avid contributors to society. Yet their fears are many, and they are so dependent on their own ability to prove their superiority and knowledge to the world that, ironically, this is the very element that trips them up.

Nobel Prize winner John Nash (captured in *A Beautiful Mind*) and the Hannibal Lector character played by Anthony Hopkins in *Silence of the Lambs* (1991) are both good examples of the Observer character taken to extremes. Psychologists agree that there is a fine line between extreme intelligence and insanity.

Your Observer characters see the world as a collection of details that are of vivid importance to themselves, inconsequential to others. They require as much praise and admiration as an Energizer, yet care only about praise directed at their keen mental abilities.

This keen mental ability isn't necessarily relegated to business, science, or technology. Observers make excellent artists, musicians, costume designers, fashion designers, jewelry designers, hairdressers, make-up artists, interior designers, and architects – in short, any field that demands complete and utter attention to the smallest detail.

The author Marcel Proust is an excellent example of an Observer, especially in the writing of *Remembrance of Things Past*, which so viscerally and visually recreates minute details of scenes, it feels as if one is watching a movie.

Observers, curiously, are incredibly emotional in the sense that it doesn't take much to send them over the edge. At their lowest point, they can come across as neurotic as the character Jack Lemmon played in *The Odd Couple* (1968). Because Observers can lose touch with reality so quickly, others around them soon learn how to push their buttons and send them over the edge.

If you recall the film, *The Odd Couple*, you will remember that Lemmon's character, Felix Unger, could burst into tears at the site of a messy room or fallen soufflé. Why? Observers pride themselves on their ability to create perfection. When a project they feel responsible for fails (whether or not it was their fault) they find it difficult to handle the emotion.

A frustrated Observer, losing touch with reality

As a group, Observers live in a world of their own creation which follows their rules. We will never know if living in an "imperfect" world set John Nash spiraling into madness, but given his personality style, it's a good bet. One can also guess that murdering his fellow human beings and eating their flesh was perfectly normal to Hannibal Lector. As the fictional actress Norma Desmond would say "I was always big! It's the pictures that got small!"

Observers break down when the world does not live up to their personal vision of how it should run. The degree to which they break down depends on the severity of the failure and their own mental state. Many Observers are solid citizens who are able to keep themselves in check. But if you create an Observer as a key character, realize that you should create a few scenes in which he struggles with his emotions and actively tries to get a grip on himself.

Observers must consciously "self talk" their way to sanity. When Movers hit an obstacle or blow a deal, they may be upset but their natural confidence enables them to move forward and get over it.

Observers are cocksure, rather than confident, and more temperamental. When things don't go the way they've laid them out to go in their minds, frustration and panic set in.

Understanding Character Attraction

As in real life, what characters need, and what they desire, are often two different things. In *Chinatown*, the sexual attraction between Gittes and Mulwray was strong. While their personality types were well suited, their social positions were not, especially for the long term. While Evelyn Mulwray could handle it, Gittes wasn't the type of man who'd allow himself to be effectively kept by a wealthy woman his social superior.

A similar scenario of a controlling male Mover in love with a wealthy, sophisticated woman arises in the film *Blood and Sand* (1941), starring Rita Hayworth as the aristocratic Dona Sol and Tyrone Power as Juan Gallardo, the successful bullfighter from the barrio. As a Mover, the married Juan saw Dona Sol as a challenge to overcome and a wild, sensual woman to be tamed. Like all Movers, he has absolute confidence he could win her, and he did for a time, thanks to his success in the ring. Yet unlike Evelyn Mulwray, Dona Sol was an Energizer who quickly bored with toys – including Juan. Thrown by his inability to keep his prize, Juan spiraled into a tailspin that ended with his life.

When Mover and Energizer romantic leads first meet, it should be as if thunder is clashing in the background. The lust should be almost palpable. This was successfully accomplished in many films, notably many of the Act 1 scenes in *Fatal Attraction* when actors Michael Douglas and Glenn Close engaged in overheated looks and double-entendres during a party, a business meeting, and a restaurant dinner before throwing caution to the wind and embarking in some of the wildest, most erotic lovemaking in cinematic history at the time.

Let's take a look at how character types behave in a romantic comedy, using the film *Pretty Woman* (1990) as an example:

Initially, you might have considered Richard Gere's character, Ed Lewis, a Mover. Backstory revealed in the film that he had a history of avoiding long-term relationships with women, had a strained relationship with his late father, and delights in conquering opponents and winning the deal. These are all classic Mover patterns.

Now, if you have seen the film, try to think of the specific scene in which Gere's character proved he isn't a Mover.

If you guessed the scene in which he was willing to let go of the deal because Vivian "got through" to him and taught him a valuable life lesson, you are right. Movers do not abandon their positions, no matter what. True movers would stay in the game until they killed or were killed. This is what gives them the aura of danger and excitement so seductive to the opposite sex.

In *Pretty Woman*, Gere's character was seductive mostly because of (the actor's) looks and the character's status and money.

Consider that many films have successfully portrayed ruthless criminals in a very seductive light, when the actors playing the roles lacked Gere's exceptional looks or class.

Why? Perhaps it goes back to the old saying, "ladies love outlaws."

Whether the Mover is a man or a woman (Sharon Stone portrayed a Mover in the film *Basic Instinct* [1992]), the bottom line is that they stop at nothing to get what they want.

In *Pretty Woman*, Ed Lewis didn't even realize he wanted Vivian in his life until nearly the last reel. While this makes for a happy ending and big box office success, it clearly demonstrates he is not a Mover.

Ed Lewis is an Observer.

Typical of the breed, he's divorced himself from "needing anyone." Unlike the Mover prototype, he has real and imaginary fears – namely, a fear of heights. He's carefully structured his world on always being right. In one scene, he tells Vivian he outwitted his father in a key business deal. One can only imagine what intense pleasure this would bring the Observer personality style.

As a red-blooded male, it's understandable how Ed Lewis would find Vivian attractive. Yet at the same time, sex wasn't on his mind at the time of their meeting (it would have been for a Mover). Instead, he simply wanted the "right way" to reach his hotel in an unfamiliar city in an unfamiliar car. Also, it's unlikely that a Mover would ever stop the car to ask directions, especially of a woman.

Until the end of Act 1, there is no "love at first sight" nonsense between the characters. We see Ed Lewis display the first moment of tenderness when he sees Vivian sleeping in bed for the first time without her cheap blond wig, and he murmurs "you're beautiful." Yet even as he says the words, there is no emotion behind them.

Vivian's persona is that of an Energizer. As a young, confused, abused teen, she's not yet consciously aware that a better life can be hers. Yet note how easily she slips into a high-style life of fame with beautiful clothes and famous, powerful friends. Vivian's built-in Energizer qualities make it easy to upgrade her lifestyle in the course of a few days.

Of all the personality styles, Energizers (natural actors all) find it impossibly easy to shrug off one lifestyle and slip on the new, like a just-bought dress. They are highly adaptable, and easily swing to the next rung on the social ladder. Friends are important to the Energizer only as long as they are useful to them.

Consider Vivian's behavior had she possessed a Relater personality style.

First, because Relaters are needy and consciously or subconsciously seeking love in every interaction, the relationship-phobic Ed would have been so eager to get rid of her after paying her for sex he would not have made the week-long offer to stay with him.

Second, if she miraculously lasted until the end of Act 2, when Ed asks her to be his mistress, Vivian – as a Relater – would have jumped at the chance. With a condo and home base, she'd feel needed and loved.

Do the above illustrations shed light on how carefully you must consider your characters' personality types?

This section opened explaining that the quick-to-burn passion of the Mover/Energizer or Energizer/Energizer personality style combinations makes for great sex scenes but little hope for happily-ever-after at story's end.

Observer/Energizer matches, though slower to catch fire, have built-in staying power.

The previous examples also should cue you in to the fact that each of the four basic styles functions at different levels. *Pretty Woman's* Ed Lewis was an example of a "healthy" Observer style.

To showcase the similarities and differences of the Energizer style, let's look at two female Energizers about the same age, the character of "Vivian" in *Pretty Woman* and the character of "Penny Lane" in the film *Almost Famous* (2000).

Before we discuss these two styles, in your mind or on paper, consider how they are similar and how they are different.

Unconsciously or consciously, both women sought to be the "star" by associating themselves with people (namely, men) who already had the celebrity or power their personality style appreciated, valued, and craved.

Throughout much or most of history, women traditionally attained a position of power and measure of their own "spouse stardom" by associating themselves with people (men) who would give them platforms in society. Presidential First Ladies attained "fame" simply by being wives of famous men.

Today, even though more options are available to them, many women see men as stepping stones to fame. Though talented in her own right, Mariah Carey's marriage to high-powered music executive Tommy Mattola certainly jump started her career.

By contrast, Madonna (a primary Mover with strong Energizer qualities) attained fame on her own. The key difference, one might speculate, between Madonna and Mariah is that Madonna had a strong sense of mission and inexhaustible self-confidence that had little to do with her looks or her voice. She firmly saw herself in the seat of power, and set out to attain her goal. Had her focus been real estate instead of music, she'd be Manhattan's new real estate mogul today. Yet like every Mover, she took a careful inventory of her skills and made the most of what she had.

Plotting Character Attraction with Personality Styles

Before you can create character conflicts you must consider the laws of attraction. In the fictional world – just as the real world – we judge others in just three to 10 quick seconds. In that time, we make snap judgments of others that are not easily reversed.

Oscar Wilde said "It is only shallow people who do not judge by appearances. The true mystery of the world is the visible, not the invisible."

Consider how you judge people when you first meet them. Before they open their mouths, you may be:

- ✓ Looking at their appearance;
- ✓ Noting their age;
- ✓ Observing their grooming;
- ✓ Sizing up their clothing;
- ✓ Subconsciously assessing their socioeconomic level;
- ✓ Deciding if they are "above you" or "below you" in class and appearance;
- ✓ Determining (before they speak) if they seem trustworthy;
- ✓ Deciding if it's worth introducing yourself and getting to know them;
- ✓ Planning a potential escape.

All of the above assessments are made even before your character speaks.

Consider two thought-provoking films. They are *The Shop Around the Corner* (1940) and its modern remake, the Tom Hanks and Meg Ryan vehicle, *You've Got Mail* (1998).

In both films, the two eventual lovers knew one another yet had no idea the person they dismiss or despise in real life is actually their secret correspondent. The writer's goal was to dismiss appearance from the relationship, and have the two characters fall in love via correspondence. Since both sets of characters from the films knew and despised one another, part of the fun was seeing sworn enemies fall in love.

Personality Styles and Romance

In the real world, your characters will judge one another on appearances. Let's speak of the fictional world, where we now have the tools to create innovative plot twists and conflicts via personality style.

The examples below are focused on male/female romantic relationships. What about buddy pictures, you might ask? Or a dramatic heist film? Or a coming of age story? And how about a mystery or thriller?

Read the following passage with your particular story in mind. One of the most enjoyable aspects of a heist picture, for example, is seeing the dynamics of the men in the criminal gang. There is always a leader. Typically, he is a Mover. There is his crew. Fill the crew with one of each of the four types, if possible, and use the discussion below to show potential conflicts between the Mover and each of his crew members. Quentin Tarantino's *Reservoir Dogs* (1992) is a great example of this.

Buddy pictures have dynamics very similar to male/female relationships. Think of the classic film *Butch Cassidy and the*

Sundance Kid (1969). Both characters were likeable, but one did all the masterminding.

Even in buddy pictures, room for just one Mover

The Male Mover

When trying to find a female personality style that would suit your male Mover, realize that the "best" female personality style is one that custom fits the most pressing needs of your Mover.

The Male Mover... with the Female Observer Personality Style

Some Movers would appreciate a female Observer mate, since the woman's attention to detail would keep them on track and free to focus on other aspects of their business. Many real-world entrepreneurs choose Observer mates for this reason and regard them as their most valuable employees.

This is usually a long-lasting relationship because with both these personality styles, there are few surprises. Each knows what is expected of the other and work symbiotically together toward a common goal. Of course, there is little passion after the initial romantic fireworks.

If this relationship is central to your story, you may have trouble finding innovative plot twists outside issues of fidelity or betrayal. Even so, realize that, by nature, the female Observer is not a particularly emotional creature.

The Male Mover... with the Female Mover Personality Style

Male/Female Mover relationships are more like a business transaction than a marriage. Though neither is particularly emotional, each is determined to be the boss, so the relationship is bound to have issues of control.

Any sexual relationship this couple has will show strain after the Honeymoon, because the competitive thrill that might have initially stoked the romantic fire could be transformed into a vendetta as both sides fight for control of the relationship.

This marriage is often short lived, as marital competition will take its toll on the Mover's real focus, which is work. If the marriage does survive it is because both parties view the marriage as their private corporation and seek romance with others.

The Male Mover... with the Female Relater Personality Style

Many male Movers appreciate the female Relater because she brings warmth and heart to his cold, structured world. Relaters are also listeners, and Movers love to talk, so each party clearly fulfills the need of the other.

Here are some potential conflicts in male Mover/female Relater situations:

✓ The Relater becomes needy, especially when over time she sees that the Mover's true passion is his work. Frustrated and unable to deflect the Mover from his work objectives, the marriage dissolves.

✓ As the Relater is easily conquered, the male Mover seeks new challenges.

The Male Mover... with the Female Energizer Personality Style

Male Movers are attracted to female Energizers who are full of life and bring fun to the relationship. This is one of the best combinations of personality styles for generating real fireworks, conflicts, and drama. Think of the historic billionaire William Randolph Hearst and former chorus girl Marion Davis.

Many a seductive Energizer will stay with a Mover as long as he is at the height of his power, but when the power is gone, so is she.

The Male Energizer

When trying to find a female personality style that would suit your male Energizer consider the Energizer's twin needs of constant stimulation and an audience to appreciate him.

The Male Energizer ... with the Female Observer Personality Style

Look in the real world for Energizer examples and you will notice many are married to Observer personality types. Energizing Males, even more than male Movers, need women to keep them in line. Actor Robin Williams is an Energizer, and from newspaper accounts about his second wife she seems to fit the Observer profile.

Energizer men appreciate that female Observers calculate responses before resorting to wild shows of emotions. For example, if an Observer female found her Energizer male to be unfaithful (not uncommon considering the Energizer's need for attention and adoration), she would consider the benefits and risks of bringing the subject up in the first place. A female Observer often takes on the role of "mother" in this relationship, allowing the Energizing male to be a bad boy and still offer unconditional love.

Unions are successful as long as the Observer sees that she has more to gain by staying married than divorcing.

The Male Energizer ... with the Female Mover Personality Style

Female Movers can form symbiotic relationships with Energizing Males. Similar to the personality style of Observers within the scope of marriage, Female Movers serve both as business managers and executive secretaries to their mates. Often, the female Mover is the preferred personality style of gay or bi-sexual Energizing males who want both strong women at their backs and the semblance of heterosexual relationships.

For Energizing males, the qualities offered by female Movers and female Observers can be blurred. Both these personality styles offer a forgiving mother figure who looks at any situation in a more rational fashion than the Energizer personality style is capable of, and makes few personal demands. The key difference is that the female Observer is the more passive partner, quietly listening and assessing a situation, whereas the female Mover tends to be more vocal and strident in what the Energizing male should do to improve his situation.

If actor Michael Douglas is an Energizer, consider Catherine Zeta-Jones his Mover wife.

The Male Energizer... with the Female Relater Personality Style

At first glance, you may consider the female Relater to be a good mate to the Energizer. Points in the female Relater's favor are that she will likely remain in awe of her Energizer mate for her entire life, and treat him like his number one fan. Unlike the male Mover, male Energizers don't mind being smothered in love.

Female Relaters really enjoy doing small acts of kindness for their Energizer mates, and male Energizers enjoy the attention. Male Energizers don't mind the Relater's deep-seated need to be loved and constant reassurance of affection. As the male Energizer considers small compliments and his genial nature to be the tools of his trade, he makes sure everyone – including his Relater wife – feels loved and cared for when in his presence.

The Male Energizer ... with the Female Energizer Personality Style

This Energizer-Energizer union is the least likely marriage to succeed, quickly marked by jealousy (professional or otherwise) and an escalating sense of competition. Energizers, whether male or female, have a deep rooted need to be the stars of the show. Everyone else in their life is a supporting player.

The Male Observer
When trying to find a female personality style that would suit your male Observer, consider that the Observer gives long and careful thought before allowing roots to settle in any relationship.

The Male Observer... with the Female Mover Personality Style
In real life, it's not uncommon for Observers to choose Mover mates. The type of Observer man who does so is quieter than his wife, who is the dominating personality in the marriage. Since the Mover and Energizer styles are the most logic-oriented of the four personality styles, the Observer male appreciates his Mover consort's common sense. He also appreciates the way she makes things happen, rather than charting them out or theorizing about success.

An interesting psychological component to this relationship is that the Observer could feel threatened and diminished by his wife's intelligence and drive. She manifests successes he can only dream about because he won't implement any change until he has performed appropriate research. And for an Observer, there's no end to the amount of research that can be performed and tested. Movers "just do it."

The Male Observer... with the Female Observer Personality Style
Birds of a feather flock together, and this is true of the Observer-Observer relationship. They feel comfortable with one another since they have the same methodological approach to any situation. They appreciate the "no surprises" aspect of their relationship, and can be quite content with one another.

As you might imagine, they are not lively guests at a chic dinner party.

The Male Observer... with the Female Relater Personality Style

This is the perfect relationship for insecure Observers (even though they puff their chests with their academic or professional accomplishments, they remain insecure in other areas of life) who want wives who appreciate their vast intelligence. A strong Observer character may feel threatened by a Mover, and prefers the more traditional style of woman who functions as his support system.

The Male Observer... with the Female Energizer Personality Style

Powerful male Observers can and do attract female Energizers who enjoy the Observer's adoration and advice. The male Observer who has achieved monetary and professional success sees the Energizing female as a physical sign that he's "made it."

Male Observers are very careful about appearances, so their Energizer mates would be attractive but never cross the boundary into impropriety.

Of all the relationships, this is the most dynamic for character conflict. Trouble can start in this relationship for a variety of reasons, but the two key reasons would be if the male Observer loses his power base, or if the female Energizer's behavior crosses the line. Social disgrace is the key thing that the male Observer will not tolerate.

The Male Relater

When trying to find a female personality style that would suit your male Relater, remember that the Relater is a warm, touchy, feely kind of person who requires constant assurance he is loved.

The Male Relater... with the Female Mover Personality Style
Female Movers prefer male Relaters who make it possible for them to concentrate on their work. Male Relaters are understanding mates who appreciate strong women. What they appreciate most about female Movers is their quick decision making ability and logical nature.

The Male Relater... with the Female Observer Personality Style
As is the case with the female Mover, the female Observer gives a sense of logic and structure to the Relater's world. Problems can easily arise because of the Observer's cold nature. Not particularly affectionate by nature, the Relater will have a hard time getting his female Observer mate to "open up" emotionally and physically.

The Male Relater... with the Female Relater Personality Style
Relater-Relater relationships can work out because both parties are affectionate and in the best scenario, fill one another's needs. Economically, they may lag behind their peers because of severe decision making issues, combined with the fact they are usually last to jump on any forward-moving economic bandwagon.

Observing the World Around You
Keep your notebook with you and begin to record the dynamics all around you, from the pecking order and conflicts that develop at work to squabbles at family reunions. Analyze your friends. Try to figure out what "type" they are, the type they married, and guess why. (Advice: do not let your friends know you are doing this!)

In your notebook, you quickly will see your characters' personalities taking shape. You will now understand why they are
attracted to people and projects, and what motivates them to
action. You will recognize fears they don't even realize they
have, and you will pave the way to a successful story.

◆ CHAPTER SUMMARY ◆

In this chapter you learned:

1. All successful screenplays and novels are about relationships between characters.

2. You can recognize the Mover personality style by his "fight to the finish" attitude.

3. You can recognize an Energizer character by his need to be in the limelight.

4. You can recognize a Relater by his need to be loved and appreciated.

5. You can recognize an Observer by his need to logically work out every situation in his mind before he acts.

6. When Mover and Energizer characters first meet, thunder claps. This is the most dynamic of all relationships.

◆ ASSIGNMENTS ◆

1. See a feature film and, afterwards, determine the personality styles of the key characters. Analyze if they worked together well, and how the story might have been different if characters were of different types.

2. While you are watching a new film, quickly analyze the lead character, but in your mind, pretend he's another type. Notice how his actions and the scenes no longer make sense.

3. Analyze the personality style of your friends. Consider the choices they've made in life, and try to assign some pattern to the personality styles based on your personal experience

♦ CHAPTER THREE ♦

HOW TO SUMMON CHARACTERS FROM THEIR MAGICAL SPHERES

As you discovered in the last chapter, the right balance of personality types is of key importance in your novel or screenplay. The More-Personality system, based on ancient methods of personality typecasting, allows you to tap into archetypes and popular personality profiles to sharpen your existing characters and add conflict, subplots, and tension to your story.

Now, we will focus on more esoteric ways of developing your characters. Many writers first find the plot or story idea, and then fashion a character to fit the demands of the story. Others draw freely on people they meet in everyday life for inspiration and form composite characters.

Yet an equal number of writers I've interviewed "receive" their characters fully formed, as if they had traveled from a different planetary sphere or dimension.

Award-winning author Ray Bradbury reveals that his characters come to him each morning as he is just beginning to awaken. They introduce themselves and their stories. Then, all Bradbury has to do is write down their words. In my television interview with Helen Fielding, she revealed that Bridget Jones manifested to her, fully formed.

In a similar fashion, a *New York Times* magazine feature reported that the famous "Eloise" character was born when its author, Kay

Thompson, apropos of nothing, suddenly said "I am Eloise. I am six years old and live at the Plaza Hotel," while rehearsing with her jazz band.

When I read how Eloise was created, it reminded me of Shirley MacLaine's book, *Out on a Limb*, which revolved around the practice of "channeling." MacLaine spoke about channeling in the form of receiving information from other entities and spirits residing on different planetary/dimensional spheres. The thought suddenly came to me: *if spirits can be channeled, why not characters?* And is it possible that characters who suddenly come to us are not figments of our imagination, but actual beings residing in a different dimension?

Even if you don't personally believe that characters exist, fully formed, in another dimension, for the sake of your writing career, try to be open to this as a possibility. When you "manifest" characters from another dimension, they are charged with energy all their own, and instantly attract and engage all who see them.

Why do characters manifest in the first place? Possibly because they want to achieve immortality on the printed page or frame of celluloid. Or, more seriously, because they see the need to act as role models or bring humans to a new awareness or level of understanding.

In many respects, the character Julia Roberts played in *Pretty Woman*, Melanie Griffith played in *Working Girl* (1988), and Renée Zellweger played in *Bridget Jones's Diary* (2001) served as effective role models for issues women struggled with at the time.

You may question how a prostitute elevating herself to becoming a rich man's wife, as is literally the case in *Pretty Woman*, can be seen as a role model. Consider that the target audience never really pictured Roberts' character as a prostitute, but rather, the archetype of a down-on-her-luck young woman with a vivacious personality and intelligence who, thanks to fate, gets a fresh start in life. This motif is not unlike the archetype represented by the character and film *Rocky* (1976), in which the underdog emerges triumphant.

Hearing Voices & Seeing Entities

So, you might ask, how does one master the art of manifesting characters – of drawing them down from the mysterious plane in which they reside, and coaxing them to life on the page or screen?

Ask a dozen authors how they discover their characters, and you will get a dozen answers. If I, personally, were asked to define "channeling," I'd give a simple answer: it is the ability to connect with beings from another space, time, or dimension.

However, the world's leading physicists would explain the channeling concept in a scientific, highly mathematical formula (the time-space continuum).

The foundation of the time-space continuum begins with Pythagoras (remember high school geometry?) who defined a triangle as $[a^2 + b^2 = c^2]$ where a, b, and c are the lengths of the sides of the triangle and continues with Einstein's theory of Relativity, which states that neither time, length, or mass remain constant addictive quantities when approaching the speed of light.

Scientists theorize that our ideas of time and space come from the fact we are accustomed to living in a three dimensional universe – but that other dimensions exist. I encourage you to read more about the foundation for the space-time continuum at *http://dmoz.org/Science/Physics/Relativity/Time_Travel/*

As writers, let's consider "channeling" a way of bringing the characters in our subconscious mind to physical form as characters in a script or novel.

Produced screenwriter/novelist Allison Burnett is inspired by dreams and needs to hear his character's voice before writing. Once he can hear the characters and see the characters, he simply transcribes their words as if he were a channeler.

"If a Martian came down and saw a writer in his study, clicking symbols on a keyboard for hours on end, completely immersed in the world of his story, he might think it was a psychotic activity," notes Burnett, who believes the secret of creating dazzling characters is to combine that "channeling" with craft and technique to shape and texture and structure it later. "During the revision period, I'm objective and detached, simply doing the technical work," he says.

Burnett recalls that the voice of B. K. Troop, the unemployed, middle-aged, bipolar, gay, bitingly witty, erudite, unattractive narrator of his novel *Christopher: A Tale of Seduction* reached out to him first, followed by visualization of Troop's physical appearance, and then the story plot. Burnett recalls that in the creation and writing of the novel there were times that he felt he was "going off his rocker" and living in an alternative universe.

The Collective Unconscious

Technically, the Collective Unconscious is a theoretical construct of Carl Jung, who believed that all human beings have access to the collected mental experience of all their ancestors and that these memories (in symbolic forms) are carried genetically from one generation to the next.

In his book *Real Magic,* author Isaac Bonewits expands on Jung's theory by weaving it into his own theory of the "Switchboard," which suggests that there is a network of interlocking metapatterns of everyone who has ever lived or who is living now, expressed as constantly changing and infinitely subtle modifications of current telepathic transmissions and receptions.

Interestingly, Bonewits' theory goes on to say that "phenomena interpreted as spirits may be actually circuits within this Switchboard" – which means that the life experiences of every individual who has ever lived are part of our genetic encoding.

According to Bonewits and the philosophers he studied, every human being is constantly broadcasting and receiving on telepathic wavelengths. This may explain the experience you might have had if you thought of a friend only to have the friend ring you a moment later.

If you can believe that every human has the memories of every living human being, as well as all the memories of those who are now dead buried deep within their memories, then the next step is figuring out how to tap into this potentially rich resource for better characterization.

Scientists have proven that when we first meet a new human being, we receive over a hundred different non-verbal messages per second. That's right... a hundred different messages per second.

This activity takes place in the limbic section of our brain, the area which directs appetites and urges that help our species survive. In cavemen days, our limbic system directed the "fight or flight" response to situations that could pose a threat to our survival.

In a fight or flight situation, our limbic system kicks into action when approached by a stranger, quickly noting non-verbal cues such as a smile (friend?) or the grasping of a rock (enemy!) to let us know which action to take. Though we've advanced from caveman days, our limbic system is still active in situations like walking down a dark alley or meeting a competitor, face to face.

Remember times when you took an instant like or dislike to someone for no apparent reason. Chances are, it was your limbic system silently taking non-verbal cues into account, and also, subconsciously scanning appearance, tone of voice, and other nonverbal messages against similar types of people you have personally met in the past or have experienced in a film or on television.

While Jung's theory of the Collective Unconscious may never be proven and it's doubtful scientists can ever prove the theory of the Switchboard, we can take advantage of these philosophies to empower and sharpen our character-writing skills.

Channeling & Tapping into the Power of Our Own Minds

Reports of oracles and prophecies date back before Greek and Roman mythology, and the Bible is filled with references of mediums receiving communication from and about supreme beings.

Is it possible that there is an alternative universe where characters live, and use writers as vessels to be transformed to the written page or celluloid image?

Oscar Levant wrote that he doesn't believe in God, but still prays every night, just in case.

In the same way, it's imperative that even if you "don't really believe" that characters exist on a parallel universe and use you, the writer, as a tool to give them the spark of life via words and pictures, you must convince yourself that this is true.

In our conversation, Allison Burnett stressed over and over that he enters the world of his characters so deeply he becomes almost autistic, and gives himself up to something that resembles automatic writing (which is sharpened later in the editing phase).

While working at various studios, I've notice that it was common for production companies to come up with similar stories or characters simultaneously. Yet curiously, produced screenwriter David Tausik (*Driving Me Crazy* [1991] and more) tells me that both he and a classmate independently came up with the same idea of a horrific family reunion in 6th grade when their teacher gave them an assignment.

Years later, they met up with one another at Brown and independently moved to Los Angeles within a week of one another. They are now writing partners, though the horrific family reunion, so far, isn't on their list of projects.

This story aroused my imagination. Could it be that there is a family on a different plane, using both David and his schoolmate as a vehicle to be drawn down to our world in the form of a story?

Are Your Characters Imprisoned in Your Mind – or Computer?
Have you seen Michelangelo's Sistine Chapel fresco in which God touches the hand of Adam, bringing him to life? As creator of your characters, you are the god who gives your characters the divine spark. Until you make this connection, your characters

are imprisoned inside your mind or your computer's hard drive.

Conceptually, it's similar to the way writers and artists relied on the muse to give their work the divine spark of life. Some writers "live" with their characters trapped inside them for years, unable to bring (or channel) them into the physical world.

My goal, then, is to give you the tools to "channel" or draw your character down to the printed page.

Altered States

Allison Burnett described his process of voiding his mind completely and letting his characters enjoy free reign of his mind and senses. David Tausik speaks his characters' dialogue as he writes or even thinks about them in public as a way of entering their universe. UCLA Screenwriting professor Lew Hunter, screenwriter and author of *Lew Hunter's Screenwriting 434*, likes to spend the first few minutes after waking to simply lie in bed, look at the ceiling, and let his mind wonder to the world of his characters.

Harlan Ellison says that when he enters the world of his story and examines possibilities, it's as if ideas were bubbling beneath the ooze of a "hallucinatory swamp" where notions or visions would bloop to the surface. He would take the most useful concepts and put them to use.

The first step, then, is to get yourself into an altered state through meditation, self-hypnosis, prayer, exercise, or other activity that takes you out of the "real world" and into an inner reality.

Once you find what works for you, ritualize the activity. The more you practice the activity and success you experience as a result (in terms of improved focus and productivity), the easier it will be for you to access the world of your characters.

The right mental state allows David Lynch (*Mulholland Drive* [2001], *Blue Velvet* [1986]) to make deeper connections with his characters and story. Lynch does not type his screenplays, but rather, gets into a comfortable space (physically and mentally) and transcribes the action to a friend or assistant at the computer keyboard.

In this way, he is free to see the story tumble out as if a dream. Clearly visualizing the scene as he speaks of it, and hearing the character's voice, is paramount.

Creativity Is Stimulated by Joy and Laughter

Perhaps you've experienced enhanced creativity after seeing a funny film or reading a juicy story. You raced to the computer energized, and in minutes were amazed to discover yourself typing away at the keyboard, unaware of the passage of time as ideas and clever snippets of dialogued flowed from your brain through your fingers to the keys and inside the computer.

Research suggests that the creative right brain is stimulated by laughter and fun. Technically, the reason is that laughter and leisurely, pleasurable activities put us in a relaxed state which activates neurons in the frontal, concentration-oriented area of the brain so crucial to the creative process.

Some writers define writing in flow as a period in which words fill your page, as if by magic. Wolfgang Amadeus Mozart was said to have written many of his finest works as if taking dictation, describing his mood as "being in good cheer" as he did so.

The good news is that writing in flow is possible. You know it's possible, because you've experienced it. But the question remains: how can we pump up the creative productivity in every writing session? How can we write in flow at will?

Dennis Palumbo: Psychotherapist Specializing in Creative Issues
Dennis Palumbo entered Hollywood as co-screenwriter of the award-winning film, *My Favorite Year* (1982). Today he helps writers enhance their confidence and productivity as a psychotherapist and the author of *Writing from the Inside Out* (John Wiley & Sons).

As you can imagine, Hollywood is a competitive environment, and many writers loose confidence when they see their peers getting bigger deals or garnering more buzz.

Many writers decide to work with Palumbo out of frustration, feeling as if they will never be good enough, or have developed a nagging voice that, in sum, says "who do you think you are to be writing screenplays?" or "you'll never be as good as x, y, or z."

Palumbo can relate.

When he was starting out in Hollywood he had been haunted by similar fears after he was hired to adapt a difficult novel by a famous author, and make it work as a linear screenplay.

Very quickly into the project, he became stuck.

One night, he had a vivid dream in which he was standing in a broad field while an old-fashioned bi-plane buzzed him from the air. The famous novelist was leaning out of the plane, yelling at him to grab the end. All Palumbo had to do was reach for it, but his feet were planted on the ground. "All I kept thinking was, I can't reach, it's too high, I can't…"

When Palumbo woke up, he knew immediately why he was stuck on the screenplay. He had so much respect for the author, initially he felt unworthy to adapt his novel. The dream allowed him to realize that as long as he felt this way, he couldn't do what he needed to do, namely, discard much of the middle of the book and totally remake the material for the screen.

In other words, he became stuck when a nagging voice at back of his mind said "who do you think you are to adapt this great man's work?"

Once Palumbo struggled to answer this voice, he became unstuck and the words began to flow.

Writer's block is another word for being stuck, but Palumbo feels that calling the "stuck" feeling writer's block is wrong.

"The word 'block' invites writers to break through or overcome something negative that is impeding the forward momentum of the writing. But, if our first impulse upon encountering something is to break through it, we forfeit the opportunity to examine it, to find out what it is."

So, how can you lose the negative voice and gain confidence? Palumbo offers two valuable exercises.

First, Palumbo advises writers who become scared or anxious in the process of writing a story to find a character who may be scared or anxious in the script or novel… and transfer those same feelings to that character, whether in the story itself or in the course of private dialoguing or journaling with that character. Asking the character why he feels blocked or frustrated, and carefully listening to the answers, may help uncover the reasons why you, the writer, feel blocked or frustrated.

Second, Palumbo advises writers to write a dialogue between yourself and your inner critic. The next time you hear a voice saying, "this isn't good enough" separate that voice from yourself, and consider of whom that voice reminds you. Was there an authority figure (parent, teacher) in your youth who put you down? Once you make the connection, think about how you felt and responded to this criticism when you were a child. Come to an understanding with yourself and work out feelings from the past.

Jean Raffa, author of *Dream Theatres of the Soul: Empowering the Feminine Myth through Jungian Dreamwork*, had an experience similar to Palumbo's when, at the age of 10, she started a novel based on a powerful dream. The negative voice came to her in the form of "Who do you think you are, a 10-year-old girl, to think you could possibly write a novel?"

She writes that it took her 35 years to get up the courage to write from her heart again, and discover, then conquer, the blocks via dreamwork.

Banishing Negative Emotions for Enhanced Creativity

Dr. Michael Posner of the Washington University School of Medicine has discovered that the key to writing in flow is relaxation. The enemy of creative writing is anxiety and depression.

Emotion takes place in the limbic systems of our brains. With depression, Dr. Posner speculates, the amygdala (a part of the brain) feeds negative feelings to consciousness. As a result, the prefrontal lobe of the brain pulls out long term memories that match the depressed feeling, making us melancholy. Then the anterior cingulated cortex fastens onto these memories and prevents us from shifting to anything more uplifting. The thalamus (yet another part of the brain) keeps the whole circuit alive and firing, which explains, in part, why depression lasts so long.

To cure depression and stimulate creative writing, Posner states that the amygdala must be prevented from flooding the brain with negative emotions.

This can be accomplished through meditation.

Meditation: Your Creativity Warm-up

Many of today's best selling screenwriters and novelists have long used meditation as a way to jump start their creativity. Though the term might sound "new age," meditation is simply a way to quiet your mind so that you can get into the creative flow state.

Ray Bradbury admits to quieting his mind so that he can "hear" the voices of his characters talking to him. David Lynch, director of *Eraserhead* (1977) and *Blue Velvet,* told *Time Magazine* in August 2003 he has meditated for 90 minutes, twice a day, since 1973. "I catch more ideas at deeper and deeper levels of consciousness, and they have more clarity and power," Lynch explains.

Goldie Hawn owns up to meditating for 31 years, using meditation as a way to quiet her mind and negate destructive emotions.

Asians have accepted and incorporated meditation into their lifestyle for centuries, but Western scientists have just recently developed tools sophisticated enough to see changes in brain chemistry during meditative states.

Like Dr. Posner's work with the amygdala, Professor Richard Davidson of the University of Wisconsin uses brain imaging to show that meditation shifts activity in the prefrontal cortex of our brains (behind our foreheads) from the right hemisphere to the left, suggesting that by meditating regularly, the brain is oriented to a mode of increased contentment.

"Damn Braces, Bless Relaxes," said Poet William Blake, responding to the practice of constricting ourselves to write a certain amount of words per day or a set amount of hours, subconsciously blocking the flow of creative energy which would have been ours if we had been more relaxed.

Brian Grazer, producer of the film *Splash* (1984) and many other hit films, confirms relaxation is key to creativity. He claims to have been inspired to create the blockbuster *Splash* while gazing outside at the Pacific Ocean, the blue waves mesmerizing him into deep relaxation. Suddenly, the idea came to him in a flash: suppose a man found the love of his life — but she happened to be a fish?

How to Enter the Creativity-Producing Alpha State Via Meditation

Begin by sitting or lying comfortably with eyes closed.

Now, begin to count backwards from 50, "seeing" the numbers in your mind as you count silently or aloud.

Experience what it's like to relax and let ideas flow in this state. When you are ready to come out, count to five and open your eyes. With practice, you can condition yourself to enter this state in just five seconds.

Incorporating Hypnosis in Your Meditation Session

Hypnosis is a combination of meditation, visualization, and affirmative self. You get into the hypnotic state just as you do the Alpha state. The key difference is that with hypnosis, you plan a script in advance and read that script into a tape recorder.

One of the most effective ways to hypnotize yourself is to have your "count down" on tape, and a scripted message to yourself allowing you to relax even further. The words you use are your own, but you want to relax various parts of your body, until you are almost in a sleeping mode. (The message will reach your subconscious mind, even if you are sleeping.)

Then, your message should contain affirmative language and strong visuals. If your objective is to learn more about effective traits for your character (let's call her Julie, for an example), you might write and record a script similar to the example below.

> *"You are relaxed (say your first name) and thinking about your character Julie. Stories are all about transformations, so in this session Julie will tell you more about herself, including details of her youth that have a direct impact on her limitations in the present. Overcoming these limitations is the goal of the story, so right now, let Julie show you some crucial moments from her childhood "*

At this point, you will want to pause the recording and give your subconscious mind time to see Julie as a child. The effect will be as if you are watching a movie. What's amazing about this process is that you are "passively" watching your character telling you about her past. Julie seemingly speaks of her own volition. You simply sit in that darkened theater of your mind and let Julie show you her secrets.

Sometimes a character will start to show you an image, then replace it suddenly with another image. This is fine… it could mean any number of things, including a new direction. It's in your own best interest as a creator to jot down everything you experience for later analysis.

If you are first getting started with this process, you may wonder if "you are doing it right" – or you may become concerned because your character is not showing you an image. Be positive and have faith that with repeated sessions, your character will speak.

Also be advised that sometimes, especially if you are very resist-
ant to the process, your character won't speak to you in this setting. Instead, the character will speak to you via a dream, or possibly, when you are engaged in another activity at work. Be sure
to have that notebook handy at all times so you can write the
secrets down.

Channeling Your Character Via Dialogue (Conversing with your Character)

Sometimes, characters stubbornly refuse to open their mouths.
They won't move, they won't speak… and it's frustrating.
Worse, when characters are uncommunicative, it often can lead
to the dreaded "writer's block." In a worse-case scenario, uncommunicative characters can motivate their author to drop the project entirely.

So, what's the answer?

The best weapon is to put them on the spot and simply, directly,
ask them "Why?"

Many writers find it easiest to dialogue with the characters on
the written page, instead talking to them audibly or silently.
Begin by writing your conversation as if it were a scene between
yourself, the author, and one or more of your characters.

Be as bold as you like. If you are writing about a murderer
named Jim and can't decide how he will kill his victim, just cut
to the chase and ask.

Author:

*"Hi, Jim, I'm your creator. I'm about to write the great scene when you kill
Fred, but I can't decide how you are going to do it, or where you are going
to do it. Have any ideas?"*

Character Jim:
"Do you want it to be a real action scene? My target Fred runs a Mercedes dealership. I could send a car flying through the showroom window straight at him. Glass would fly everywhere, the audience would love it – especially for film. Or, the scene could be packed with suspense. I can dress up in my cool black Prada outfit and break into his house. The scene could be especially hot if he's entertaining a girl, I pop the shot, and the girl doesn't even knew what hit him. We cut out on her scream."

Asking your character for suggestions accomplishes several things. First, it puts you, the author, into a completely separate mindset. Instead of thinking like an author who considers "his character" as an extension of himself, you suddenly find yourself thinking from the vantage point of a completely different person. Second, this technique forces you to get inside the head of your character and think as the character actually thinks, not as you would think for him.

Dialoguing with your character is a great way to channel them to the earthly plane. Novel writers will find their dialogue is now sharp as a sushi knife. Readers immediately know who's talking without the clunky "he said" attribution and can even detect the emotion behind whatever the character is saying. Screenwriters will more easily find and bring to the surface the little details that truly make for unique characterization.

Many writers find that the above exercise is an excellent way to jump-start your writing session, every time.

Meeting Your Character
Screenwriter MJ Schrimer gets into an altered state by a "virtual meeting" with her character. She describes an incident in which she was staring at the computer screen and suddenly saw a man ride up on a horse. The man took one look at Schrimer and asked: "Who are you?"

This is a twist, isn't it? Characters so real they ask who we are, instead of vice versa? When Schrimer reported this, my first reaction was that this character, secure in his own world or dimension, took a wrong turn somewhere and ended up in our physical workaday world.

Once again, whether you "really believe" that characters exist, fully formed, in another dimension is immaterial. To write dazzling characters, you absolutely must believe it, at least in the course of writing your story.

One other element that struck me about Schrimer's story is that it eerily echoed an experience a non-writer friend of mine had with his computer. When he was shutting his computer down late one night, instead of the "goodbye" message on the screen, he saw the name of his late mother.

"It's all in their imaginations," you might say with regard to Schrimer and my friend. Yet consider that a computer is run on crystals, and crystals are also the medium which psychics use to access other worlds. If characters were to manifest anywhere, a computer is a good spot.

If you are interested in exploring how to get characters to manifest in our world, at least while you are working on your story, you must first set the right conditions for this to happen.

The first step is to convince yourself that it is actually possible. If you are the least bit skeptical, forget it. The power of suggestion is everything. Second, you must learn to relax at will. Third, each morning make an affirmation that you will see your character, such as "today I will be introduced to my character. I wonder where it will be?"

Fully expect to have your character make a surprise visit in the course of your day.

Christopher Vogler, author of *The Writer's Journey*, begins his writing sessions by closing his eyes and looking inward, imagining a blank screen somewhere inside of him. He just looks to see what will come up. Sometimes, he plays out scenes to see where they will lead, and reports he gets a lot of dialogue as characters appear and begin to speak.

Another technique he finds valuable is to create a timeline of the main events in his characters' lives, including the age they became independent, what was going on in the world at major turning points in their lives, and the formative experiences that built their character. For his animated feature *Jester Till* he selected a Bruegel painting, "The Hunters in the Snow," and kept a print above his desk for the entire writing process.

The "What if" Scenario

Professor Lew Hunter recalls that Richard La Gravanese was driving on Sunset Boulevard when he saw two men in earnest conversation. One man wore an expensive, sharp looking suit, while the other wore rags. The contrast between them was so great that Gravanese couldn't get the image out of his mind, and that happenstance encounter resulted in *The Fisher King*.

The Scrapbook Effect

M.J. Rose (Author, *Flesh Tones and Sheet Music* and *The Halo Effect*) uses a scrapbook as a tool to enter the world of her character. "Once I have a "what if" idea that has legs I buy a scrapbook for the main character and before I write a word of the novel I spend about two to three months creating her life in pictures, memento's, personal artifacts, favorite poems, quotes, letters, etc. I scour antique stores for photos of long dead people looking for a shot that suggests her or his face."

"I buy a talisman — something that belongs to my main character that I can wear or keep on my desk — to connect me to this ephemeral being I have never really met. In one book it was my main character's father's watch that she wore every day. In another book it was an oval, flat, light green rock that the main character found on a walk with her lover and kept on her desk for years. I also go shopping with him or her beside me — like an imaginary friend and let the character show me what appeals."

"I also spend days — sometimes weeks — naming him or her. It seems so much of the characters' coming to life has to do with their names. I can't ever give a main character the first name of anyone I know too well because that clouds the picture. I have to see my characters moving around and living their lives behind my eyes. I watch them living their stories... and then I write it down."

M. J. Rose's notebook phoyographed by Doug Scofield

Sarah Smith, author of *The Vanished Child* and *Knowledge of Water* (both named *New York Times* notable books of the year and published in 12 languages), along with several award-winning novels, offers an equally innovative technique. "My characters have a well-thought-out life, talismans, and a wardrobe — it was fun shopping with my Hollywood princess! I tell their fortunes and listen to their music."

"I need to know their distinct ways of talking and their emotional needs. One character, Posy, dumbs down her intelligence because it takes her away from her father, whom she adores. She talks like a Valley Girl. 'Well, Shakespeare, duh!' Joe's connection with his father strengthens him, and every time he needs to be strong he drops back into his father's Yankee talk."

"I also listen to their ideas, their obsessions. My book *Chasing Shakespeares* is about people who believe Shakespeare didn't write his plays. What if a man who loves Shakespeare meets a woman who believes Shakespeare is a fraud? And what if she has the Hollywood connections to do something about it? He's going to try to stop her."

"To develop Joe and Posy's story, I had to travel with them. I walked the same streets in London that they walk, chasing Shakespeare. I took lots of pictures of London, but I also had Joe and Posy describe the scene for me. They saw different things, of course!"

As Sarah plans her characters' story, each piece of it goes on a note card. Ideas for neat scenes, bits of characteristic dialogue, and even shopping hints each have separate cards. Her photos become "cards" as well. Then she sorts them and re-sorts them, deciding which details need to go in which scenes. As she gets a scene, she clips the cards together.

"There were three separate story lines in *Chasing Shakespeares*," says Sarah. "Shakespeare's story, the life of Posy's mysterious other man, and Joe and Posy's modern-day romance. By sorting the cards, I found out I needed to tell it by location, so each scene was keyed to a place. In *Chasing Shakespeares*, as Joe and Posy travel through England, they also travel through Shakespeare's and his alter ego's lives." (Note: You can read more about Sarah's card method at *www.sarahsmith.com*)

Tarot & I Ching

Christopher Vogler, author of *The Writer's Journey*, often uses Tarot or the I Ching system to develop characters. He will do a "reading" for the character in which certain cards and symbols show up. He then interprets the symbols in terms of what he already knows about the character, to fill in the blanks. For example, he might notice that symbols of bulls and men struggling appear frequently in the cards. This tells him the character is stubborn and strong-willed and tends to get in fights. Or symbols like swords might dominate a character's reading, telling him that this is someone who suffers and causes lots of suffering because his nature is pointed and sharp. It provides him with a level of psychological complexity and randomness.

"I believe that writing should be conducted like a ritual, a magical operation, and that the desk is a kind of altar on which you offer the sacrifice of your time and attention," says Vogler. "At the beginning you should clear and clean the altar, so you can achieve concentration, a state in which there is nothing to stimulate except the subject you want to contemplate. Then you bring one object or image into the sacred space, something that is associated with character or the location, and let that act as a magnet for thoughts and feelings. All this helps me focus. I then start bringing in more and more symbols and pictures and I even draw sketches and build models of locations and props. Before long the work area is like the inside of my head, filled with the images and inspirations. But I think it's important to fix on one thing in the beginning and touch base with it throughout the process."

Art as Inspiration

Paintings can be an excellent source of inspiration. Instead of waiting for her character to strike like a lightning bolt, Saralee Etter looks to an image for creative and spiritual guidance. For the current book she's writing, she received inspiration from a portrait of famed actor David Garrick, in which the actor is shown with two women, one tall, dark, and lovely (dressed as the figure of Tragedy and the other woman small, with curly blonde hair and a mischievous smile, representing the figure of Comedy).

By studying the portrait, Etter was able to discover a library of information about the characters in her story, their backgrounds, and their desires.

Communicating with Your Character Via Diaries

If you keep a journal or diary, you know what a useful tool it can be for letting off steam, recording your goals, and analyzing your dreams. You probably also know that if others got control of it, they would know way more about you than you would feel comfortable with.

In the film, *The Swimming Pool* (2003), the "blocked" mystery writer character played by Charlotte Rampling found a diary in the room of an intriguing young girl who shared her summer home. Reading it, Rampling's character became inspired, and the diary turned into a full-blown character description that launched a best-selling book.

When you have your characters keep diaries, imagine the power you, the author, can wield over them. Suddenly, you will have secret access to their dreams and desires, their hidden fears and bitterness over past events. The diary Rampling found in *The Swimming Pool* also contained pictures, including a picture of the young girl's mother. Can you stock your character's diary with similar pictures, perhaps torn from the pages of magazines?

Diaries may be penned by hand into cardboard notebooks you would find at any drugstore, or you may wish to invest in a hardcover journal filled with blank pages, such as you can find at any bookstore. Thick drugstore notebooks that have pockets and/or divisions may be useful if you want to keep a journal for each of your characters. If you do this, I recommend assigning each character a specific color of ink so you can tell them apart at an instant. You will also feel their energy more clearly as you are writing in their diaries.

If you prefer to keep an online diary (as I do) you would do well to assign each of your characters a different computer type font. A schoolgirl might use a font with a large, flowery script font such as Lucinda Bright. A brash guy, physically short and stubby, might be characterized by the font known as Accent.

Once you've received your first flash of a character, a character diary is the best place to build on what you know. Let them vent. Let them dream. Then listen. *Listen well!*

Character

A character collage is one of the most powerful (and most fun) ways to get to know your characters on an intimate level, as well as figuratively give them the spark of life.

Participants in my screenwriting and other workshops enjoy the technique, and get an enormous amount of information about their characters from it.

Here's how it works. Gather a big stack of magazines, the more picture-oriented, the better. Have scissors, glue, and paper (or oversized poster board) available.

Next, visualize your character in your mind's eye. Ask him to reveal himself to you as you quickly (the process must be quick and automatic) flip through the magazines, looking for any image that jumps out at you. It does not have to be a person, it can be a car, a detergent, anything that strikes a chord in your subconscious mind.

Remember to work quickly, so that it is your subconscious, not your conscious, mind that is responding to the images. Tear sheets out rather than neatly cutting them – you will have the opportunity to neatly trim your images later.

When you've assembled a large stack of images, it's time to arrange them in whatever order you desire on the page.

We approached the collage from the vantage point of her character's wants, desires, and self image.

Anything goes. You can cut out headlines or words you find in magazines, or even type them on your computer in whatever font you desire and then paste the words or phrase on the page.

If you write a character diary using a specific font to represent a character, use this font on your character collage.

What you have at the end is a collage that has various human images, representing aspects of the characters or their friends/spouses/enemies, as well as material possessions the characters either own or desire, such as yachts, cars, etc. Many character collages even have representations of the characters' favorite foods, or desired habitats.

Many attendees of my workshops also like to use textures in their work, even scent. Your collage represents the world of your character and everything that is important to him. In some ways, the collage is similar to the burial chamber of a powerful Egyptian Pharaoh, who was buried with his treasures.

The moment you complete your collage, reflect on the image. In Yoga terms, make your eyes "soft" (i.e., blurry) and see the collected images as a "whole." Meditate on the image.

Now, take your journal (or any available paper) and ask each character in your collage questions. Channel your characters. Offer the character the ability to dictate his thoughts, and promise you will be a faithful transcriber. In the end, you will be amazed at the results.

Once you complete your character collage, I suggest scanning the image and using it as a screen saver for your computer, and making several copies to paste around your home or office where you can see it constantly. Possible locations include the refrigerator door, your bathroom mirror, and an area around your desk.

Why is this method so effective? Consider a framed picture of someone you love. When you first receive it, you really "see it" and the photograph has energy. But a photograph is just one facet of the personality, and if you look at it too long it becomes dead. One would have to put up a new photograph, reflecting a new aspect of the beloved person, every day of the year to consistently get a "fresh impression."

In a similar way, when you create a character collage, you create excitement and energy.

Charting Characteristics

Another technique I find useful is charting character characteristics. This can be done by hand in your notebook, in a word file, or in an Excel file (which I use).

The method in itself is simple – and highly individual.

For example, everyone notices different things meeting new individuals. I had a friend in L.A. who, for whatever reason, would always look at the shoes of people to whom she was introduced, to assess them. I find myself looking at the hair of new people, and rarely (if ever) even glance at their shoes. Others might concentrate on a person's warmth or sincerity.

Using an Excel file I listed all the possible characteristics I – or anyone else – can notice about a person. Each characteristic was given its own column horizontally. Characters were listed vertically. As an example, my list includes voice, scent, energy level, designer favorites/stores (i.e., where they buy their clothes) as well as intangible items such as a recent dream, worst fear, biggest secret, significance of their jewelry, etc.

The idea for the chart was born when I realized that up to 97% of our information about others is transmitted non-verbally. Instead of focusing on what a character might say, I started to consider how characters would say it. Would they speak with confidence, or in faltering tones? What would their accents reveal about them? Notes on this would be included in the "voice" section.

Then my focus turned to scent when a woman working out alongside me at the gym smelled so strongly of soap it was as if she scrubbed herself raw. Why? Was there an incident in her childhood that mandated the necessity for absolute cleanliness? The scent was so strong I envisioned her in the shower with a hard-textured sponge, scrubbing herself until her very white skin turned pink. On another day, a woman on the Stairmaster smelled as if she marinated in a seductive, exotic perfume. *Again, why?* Their "scent" must have seemed natural to them, but inspired curiosity in me.

What characteristics you decide to list is up to you. It should consist of things that you, as an individual, regard as important clues when you meet someone new.

Observing Your Character

It's human nature to size up the personalities, socio-economic level, and education of others based on appearances. We will discuss the power of physical appearance more fully, but for now, let's focus on personality, especially with regard to how your characters habitually go about getting what they want through vocal exchanges in social interaction.

Remember that the focus of this book is viewing your characters as real people. Therefore, it's necessary that we observe how others view them in a public arena.

Listed below are three common types of individuals. This is a good time to get out your notebook (or some paper) and take your character through this exercise.

Each of the three personality types will be observing your character from his or her own point of view. The objective of this exercise is to surprise yourself (and learn more about your character) by making notations of how each personality type views your character, based on his appearance, as well as whatever other elements you want to include.

So now, imagine your character entering a cocktail party and encountering each of the three types in turn.

1. Your character meets "The compliment giver"

You've met people who always exclaim you've lost weight or look great. Ironically, these people use these words as a formality, figuring all people are trying to lose weight or want to think they look great.

Yet the truly savvy compliment givers spend a few moments of quality time figuring out *what kind of compliment* would most please the recipient. Fawning salespeople, knowing a client prides himself on his status as a physician, might address him as "doctor" and ask about his latest operation. A housewife might be asked to produce pictures of her children.

Exercise: How would an insincere, fawning compliment-giver greet your character? What would this individual think is the way to get your character on his good side through his greeting and conversational words?

2. Your character meets "The detractor"

If the compliment giver offers praise, the detractor even more eagerly relishes the opportunity to belittle people. Reasons for this include the polar opposites of a poor self-image combined with delusions of grandeur, lack of confidence, passion for malicious gossip, and just plain nastiness.

Detractors are most snide and vicious when they sense their territory is threatened. Self-trained to shoot for the kill, they have mastered the art of quickly identifying their enemies' most vulnerable areas. Once identified, they seek to put as much "verbal salt" as they can muster into the festering wound.

Exercise: If a detractor feels threatened by your character, what words would he use that would hurt your character the most? Why? Exploring this issue in detail will give you tremendous insight into your character. Some questions warranting your reflection include asking how the detractor recognized your character's vulnerability, and how your character reacts to the detractor's cutting words.

3. Your character meets "The true observer"

Do you have a friend who notices everything? The true observer is born with the ability to size up a person in an instant. Fine details such as changes in nail color or virtually invisible lint on jackets do not escape his scrutiny. The observer's sharp eyes also notice run-down heels, last season's handbag, and other small details.

Viewing your character through the eyes of a true observer will yield details that would escape the notice of ordinary mortals, including yourself.

Exercise: What does a true observer first notice about your character in a positive way (i.e., neatly trimmed cuticles). What would they criticize?

The Power of Dreams

The French surrealist poet, St. Paul Boux, would hang a sign on his bedroom door before retiring which read: "Poet at work."

A similar belief in nocturnal productivity was expressed by John Steinbeck: "It is a common experience that a problem difficult at night is resolved in the morning after the committee of sleep has worked on it."

Former Beatle Paul McCartney has said he heard the melody for his famous Beatles song "Yesterday" in a dream. Later, McCartney stated the dream was so vivid and the music seemed so familiar he first had to convince himself that he did not dream someone else's music that he had heard and forgotten.

Bobbye Terry, published author of several mystery and romance books, gets 100% of her inspiration from dreams. Recently, in her *Slam Sisters* mystery series, characters have begun to keep her awake as they fight with one another and insist on telling Terry what she should do with them.

G. Miki Hayden, the Agatha-award nominated author of *Writing the Mystery*, sold a short story to a publisher after immediately writing down a dream in which she, as an observer, saw two women locked in a struggle that resulted in murder.

Palumbo, too, says that he has many writer clients who describe having key plot points revealed to them through dreams. One client was stuck in the script, and he spent three nights dreaming the script as if watching a movie. On the fourth night, suddenly he knew what the character should do and became unstuck.

Rosemary Ellen Guiley, Ph.D., author of the book *The Dreamer's Way: Proactive Dreaming for Creativity and Healing* (Berkley Books, April 2004) has observed through research and interviews that dreaming is an important way to tap into the imagination and the archetypical realm where ideas and characters manifest.

Guiley reports that Dan Curtis, creator of the long-running soap opera *Dark Shadows* (1966 – 1971) was inspired by a dream about a young woman traveling by train to a gloomy mansion. Robert Louis Stevenson, author of the classic *Dr. Jekyll and Mr. Hyde*, was also inspired by a dream. In interviews, Stevenson stated that he had "brownies" who presented him with creative ideas in dreams, and his job was simply to write them down.

So, the key question is how can writers use the power of dreaming to get inspiration for plot and characters?

Guiley believes that programming our dreams to yield rich, creative fruit is made easier by the power of suggestion, and advises creative dreamers to tell themselves that they will have dreams that will provide them with inspiration and solutions. The important part is to write them down, as dreams are primarily symbols and must be decoded. Even the smallest fragment can be very enlightening.

"Sometimes we don't have dreams containing specific ideas, but the ideas are clear to us upon awakening," Guiley writes in *The Dreamer's Way*. "I see everything in a sharp, crystal clarity, as though an entire plan has been rolled out in front of me. "

Guiley also addresses the concept of "incubated creativity" in which we can frame a specific question for meditation prior to sleep. For example, she might ask "How can I ___?" before sleeping and will wake up with the answer.

In *The Dreamer's Way*, Guiley lists several innovative exercises to jump start your creative dream work. One involves entering a meditative state and visualizing yourself standing in front of a three-way mirror in a dimly lit, furnished room. The mirror should be positioned so that it shows periphery and background you cannot see otherwise. Look fully into your face, pay attention to detail. Then look at details revealed to the sides and to the back. Turn so that you can see your back completely in the mirror. Then face forward. While looking into your face, pay attention to details that emerge in your peripheral vision.

Make the affirmation: "Tonight the mirror of my dreams will reveal what is hidden or hard to see."

Case Studies
Spend just a few minutes on the Web site for the Association for the Study of Dreams (*http://www.asdreams.org*) and you will

be astonished by the vast number of scientific university studies (complete with charts, graphs, and other numerical verification) that show a correlation between creativity, problem solving, and dreaming.

At UCLA, I took part in a study myself, which attempted to prove the correlation between telepathy and dreams. The study involved a fellow student measuring my REM (rapid eye movement) with technical equipment and a long cord from another room so she could monitor when I entered the dream state. At that point, she was to open a sealed envelope containing four images. Her job was to focus on the images, even sketch them, so that she could transmit them to me in my dream. When my REM suggested I was leaving the dream state, she would buzz me. I was to wake up and write my dream.

When I saw distinct correlations between my dream and the images, I was not surprised. Like many of the writers I interviewed who used dreams as a way to get inspiration for their novels and screenplays, I've had prophetic dreams since I was a child. To me, this confirms my own theory that beyond a creativity vehicle, dreams are a conduit, or tunnel, between two or more worlds. In the dream state we can glimpse other realms and explore other realities, as well as confront our characters on a safe, neutral meeting ground.

The book *Secrets of Shamanism*, by Jose Stevens, Ph.D., and Lena S. Stevens, describes a concept in which traditional shamans slide entirely outside the present time frame in ordinary reality to bring back news of the future. The process involves meditating and leaving your physical body in this world, while traveling with your spirit body to other locations where you take care of a variety of interests. This can include meeting your character, witnessing future success (i.e., seeing positive reports of your book or script in trade publications, seeing long lines of eager fans outside the theater), etc. The Stevens note this has many advantages, especially since, when you know the probable outcome of a situation, you can plan for it in advance and set yourself up to be at the right place at the right time.

Spirit and the Unconscious Mind

Jung defines spirit as the dynamic aspect of the unconscious. Quoting from *On Divination and Synchronicity: The Psychology of Meaningful Chance*, by Marie-Louise Von Franz, "One can think of the unconscious as being like still water, a lake, which is passive. The things one forgets fall into that lake; if one remembers them, one fishes them up, but it itself does not move. The unconscious has that matrix, womb aspect, but it also has the aspect of containing dynamism and movement, it acts on its own accord – for instance, it composes dreams. Spirit, according to Jung, has the quality of freely creating images beyond our sense perception (in a dream one has no sense perception – the spirit or the unconscious creates images from within, while the sense perceptions are asleep), and there is autonomous and sovereign manipulation of those images."

Franz clarifies the above with this example. "If one looks at one's dreams, one sees they are composed of impressions from the day before. For instance, one read something in a paper, or experienced something in the street. The dream takes these fragments and makes a completely new and meaningful potpourri out of that. There one sees the sovereign manipulation of the pictures, they are put into another order and manipulated into a completely different sequence with a completely different meaning, though one still recognizes that the single elements have been taken from memory remnants of the day before.

That is why so many people think that is the whole explanation of the dream: "Oh, I read about a fire yesterday in the paper, which is why I dreamt about a fire."

Franz would advise the dreamer "Yes, but look at the connections in which the fire has been put, very different from what you read. That would be the spirit, the unknown thing in the unconscious which rearranges and manipulates inner images."

Ken Atchity, president of Atchity Entertainment International, writes in his excellent book, *A Writer's Time*, that the ancient Greek and Egyptian civilizations erected temples where troubled devotees would bring their problems to the goddesses of sleep and spend the night in the temple, awaiting revelations from the unconscious.

He advises "blocked" writing clients to gain access to the unconscious though a method of "dream incubation" involving the subconscious mind.

Atchity has devised an innovative metaphor and technique of tapping into the creative mind which he describes in detail in *A Writer's Time*. He believes that in our heads we have:

1. Many "Islands of consciousness"
2. The Continent of Reason
3. The Managing Editor

"The Islands are free-floating and changeable," Atchity writes, "but the Continent is relatively stationary and immovable. Like the Continent, each island perceives life entirely with its own fully developed viewpoint. Originality and individuality are island characteristics; the Continent is consensus of society and culture, and constructed by our education.

The Continent operates by analogy, comparing the new to what it knows already. While a new island can be formed instantly from a new impression, the Continent is slower, having to search its warehouse of memory to find a category to which to relate the new impression, so that it can use that new impression in dealing with the world outside the mind.

During sleep, the "Managing Editor" reviews all new impressions, both of new Islands (accounting for "nonsense" dreams) and ones added to the Continent's ever-expanding web of analogies (reasonable dreams)."

If you are blocked or can't figure out what your character should do next, Atchity advises you – through your "Managing Editor" – to set up an assumption before you go to sleep (i.e., Valerie has a secret she's not revealed to me yet).

The secret, says Atchity, is in the Islands. "Your Managing Editor incubates a dream, sending a telegram to the Islands and asking for a response: *What's Valerie's secret?*"

Atchity reports that dreams will provide an answer, but cautions that dream language is the language of metaphor instead of logic. "One novelist client receives entire scenes vividly spelled out when she follows this process," says Atchity, "others receive only glimpses of the barrier that's been holding them back. The longer this practice is followed and the more confidence you have in it, the more fruitful it becomes."

Of course, it is essential to write down and remember your dreams. Atchity suggests:

1. Prepare your recording devices so they are close at hand when you wake up.
2. Make sure you are not going to be awakened artificially (i.e., if you must use an alarm clock, set it to a classical station)
3. Before going to bed, tell yourself you are going to remember your dream.

4. Upon awakening, "set" the dream in your mind, notably by focusing on it and ignoring other thoughts as you set about recording it.

Beyond Dreaming

A few decades ago, a popular advertising slogan asked: "Is it live – or is it Memorex." The idea was to show that the quality of tape (this was before digital) was so superior a listener couldn't tell if the music were performed live or had been recorded.

Author Kate Flora, president of *Sisters in Crime* and best-selling author of several mysteries starring the character Thea Kozak, says: "When I write characters, I often feel that they have always existed somewhere 'out there,' and it is my challenge, as a writer, to find and discover them, through writing about them."

Characters have their own personalities, insist a number of interviewed writers, and resent you, their creator, for trying to direct them. They even resent you for trying to "catch them" when they first tantalize you by appearing to you in a dream.

Rosemary Ellen Guiley, Ph.D., states that "dreams like to present imagery or action that metamorphoses into more developed ideas in waking consciousness."

The 1947 film *The Ghost and Mrs. Muir* is an excellent example of this process, as it works on a number of levels. A romantic-suspense, the story concerns a young widow who takes a seaside home even though it's rumored to be haunted. In the first act, she meets the sea captain ghost, and as a way of helping her support herself, dictates his life story to her (*Blood and Swash: The Unvarnished Story of a Seaman's Life*), which she sells and it and becomes a best-selling book.

Near the third act, when the ghostly captain realizes their (platonic) romance is keeping her from romance with a mortal man, he causes her to pretend that his existence was all a dream, and she wrote the book herself.

The ghost makes Mrs. Muir believe he's a figment of her imagination

Our goal, then, is to open ourselves up to the forces of our subconscious mind and make a deep, emotional connection with our characters who, like the sea captain, may not exist on our Earthly physical plane.

◆ CHAPTER SUMMARY ◆

In this chapter you learned:

1. You know you are successful when readers or an audience can't stop thinking about your characters when the movie or book has ended.

2. Many of our culture's best-loved and remembered characters are archetypes.

3. Consider that channeling is a way of bringing characters from your subconscious mind to the physical, printed plane.

4. It's possible we hold the collective experience of everyone who's ever lived in our minds – and we have access to this information.

5. Creativity is stimulated by joy and laughter.

6. Meditation is an excellent way to relax to the point your character will feel comfortable entering the physical plane.

7. Consider incorporating hypnosis into your meditation session.

8. Keep a character diary for each of your major characters, individualizing the diary by a different color pen or style of font.

◆ ASSIGNMENTS ◆

1. Tell your subconscious mind to look for an image (it can be an advertisement, a painting, even a comic strip) that will give you information about the characters in your story. When you discover this image, try to reproduce it and spend time meditating on it. Often, images can speak louder than words.

2. In your next writing session, try to visualize the characters you are writing about in the room with you. Try to actually "see" them and note their actions. Do they push one another aside to see what you're writing about them?

3. Have a cup of coffee with your characters at Starbucks. Bring a pad of paper and look directly at them as you ask them questions about their past and their hopes for the future. Since conflict is essential, also ask them about the characters they like and hate in the story, and why. *Be prepared to write fast!*

4. If you have never meditated, consider taking a class on the subject at a community center or health club.

5. Ask one of your characters to write at least one entry in his diary. Analyze what you learned as a result.

◆ CHAPTER FOUR ◆

TECHNIQUES TO DISCOVER YOUR CHARACTER'S INNER WORLD

Now that we understand techniques successful writers use to manifest characters to our Earthly plane through dreams and other means, let us focus on ways to get to know your characters even better by discovering their "inner worlds."

In the film *Queen of the Damned* (2002), an attractive librarian finds the secret journal of the vampire Lestat and spends the film seeking him out as she delves into his private life and thoughts, inciting our own curiosity of what he is actually like and what will happen when they meet. She represents the viewer in that as she learns about the various, character-altering episodes of Lestat's life and personality, so do we.

To be effective, a character must be an enigma. *A mystery.* The key element distinguishing the infamous stripper Gypsy Rose Lee from prettier burlesque dancers were her elaborate props and teasing manner as she revealed herself, one layer at a time. If she stood on stage nude as soon as her number began, the audience would be cheated out of the *fun of anticipation*.

Keep this example in mind as you introduce your characters to the audience. Too much too soon, as described above, is a turn-off. *Audiences want to be seduced.* As a writer, it is your responsibility to introduce your characters in a way that arouses the audiences' curiosity. You want them to lean forward in their chairs, tension growing as they try to figure out who your character is and what makes that character tick.

Sharon Stone played such a character in *Basic Instinct*, baffling the audience, Michael Douglas, and the cops who couldn't figure her out. Ellen Barkin played a similar character in *Sea of Love* (1989). Both films achieved enormous success.

A universal turn-off for agents, editors, and producers is heavy-handed backstory and an overload of description on the page. As a writer, it's understandable that you want the audience to intimately know your character as well as you do, right off the bat. After all, in real life, when you introduce a childhood friend to current friends, you are eager to tell current friends all about your childhood pal so they'll hit it off. But avoid "filling the audience in" this way when you write.

In this chapter, we'll look at various ways of introducing your character's backstory in a way that does not disrupt the action.

Getting to Know Your Character

In my seminars I have many exercises students perform in order to better understand their characters. One exercise is called *Psychic Doctor*. In it, attendees pretend they are physicians examining the nude body of an unconscious patient just rushed into the emergency ward without any identification. As is typical in these situations, the police want to identify the individuals using scars or other unusual marks.

The twist is that the doctor is psychic, so as he examines the unconscious patient, he gathers information about the patient from various wounds and surgical scars.

The great joy of leading this exercise is hearing the excited students reveal how much they learned simply by examining the scars of their characters' physical bodies.

For example, one woman realized that her male character was missing a few fingers (the result of a factory mishap) which motivated him to wear his wedding ring around his neck, showcasing, in a visual way, his affection for his wife. Another student saw a scar that was created when his character was a young boy, defending his mother whom another child called a whore.

By this point, you have a fair idea of what your character looks like, how he dresses, his favorite activities, what he does in his leisure time, etc.

If you have been taking your characters out into the real world, as you have been instructed to do, by now you also know how they behave at parties, their favorite drinks, if they're good tippers, and what they think of your home. If you visit a department store, you will know the kind of clothes that would attract their eyes, and if you are scanning the newspaper for good movies, their choices would likely be different than yours.

Are you able to answer the following questions about your character?

- ✓ Can you name a key childhood event that had enormous impact on your character's life? It's not enough to tell yourself your character had a "good" or "bad" childhood. You must vividly see an example in your mind. Maybe he witnessed his parents fighting, one nearly choking the other to death.

- ✓ Was your character popular in school? Why? What group did he hang out with? How did this group or his popularity, or lack thereof, affect the person he is today?

✓ Can you recall any of your character's dreams? Is it a recurring dream? Can you describe it? Why does your character thinks he dreams this? What is your analysis?

✓ Who was your character's first love? How does this flavor his current relationships?

You can ask and answer endless questions about your character's past. Chances are this will never come up in your story, but it's crucial that you know this history.

Why Creating a Backstory Is Necessary
No man lives on an island. We are all influenced by our interactions with others. When authors fail to think out their character's backstory properly, the character comes across as thin, stereotypical, weak, and uninteresting.

When Actors Fill in Character Backstory
Have you ever seen the popular Emmy Award-winning cable TV show, *Curb Your Enthusiasm*? Creator Larry David gives his cast the gist of what they are supposed to say in each scene, and lets them create the dialogue and add their own nuance to the story.

A similar system is used by Robert Altman in *Gosford Park* (2001), an upstairs/downstairs story involving a celebrity cast in which Altman hires technical advisors (i.e., still-living servants to wealthy families circa the 1930s) but gives his characters the freedom to create their own life histories.

Stanislavski and the "Magic If"
The daring methods mentioned above had their roots with Konstantin Stanislavski (1863-1938) who created the "Stanislavski Method of Acting."

Stanislavski had been a Russian actor who saw that the playwrights of his day did not script histories for their characters, but rather, allowed the actors to create their own back stories and play the characters accordingly. Stanislavski decided to commercialize the concept and make it a tool for directors, playwrights, and all forms of writers. Soon his "Stanislavski Method of Acting" was taught and practiced around the world.

At the heart of the Stanislavski method was the "Magic If" – a way for actors to achieve what he called "inner truth."

The key word here is "If," which lifts us out of ourselves and gives us a sense of certainty about imaginary circumstances.

Another key principle of Stanislavski's system is that all action onstage must have a purpose. For example, if a package is opened onstage it is opened because an onstage character highlighted its importance in a way related to the plot.

Let's say that an onstage character received a package, opened it, and without showing the contents of the package to the audience, expressed the opinion it was a wedding dress she'd been expecting. If she were looking forward to getting married, she would open the package joyfully, her every move filled with her good feelings on the forthcoming wedding, based on her love of her future husband and unspoken, unseen past events (backstory) reflecting her feelings on the institution of marriage.

If she felt cornered into marriage, hated her future husband, or had negative feelings about marriage, the way she unwrapped the wedding dress would reflect this feeling.

Your Character's Inner World

What does your character think about when he's not locked inside your computer? Your character views events of the story from the standpoint of how he was raised, which is to say from his socio-economic level, his education level, and the esteem in which he holds himself.

Characters can communicate without words. The act of simply dressing can say a great deal to the outside world.

Have you thought about the clothing in your character's wardrobe? Have you imagined yourself shopping as your character would shop for clothing?

If you live in an apartment in Santa Monica, for example, and shop at the mall, have you considered how your aristocratic English character of the last century would buy his clothes? Shopping is first and foremost an expression of self. What we buy is determined by our economic situation, our class in society, and on a more subliminal level, experiences that shape peculiarities in our buying habits.

Going back to Stanislavski's method, let's assume your character grew up poor. As a small boy he was envious of the expensive looking shoes on the feet of gentleman whose shoes he polished at a stand. How would this shape his shoe-buying experience as an adult?

The famous actor the world knows as Cary Grant was actually born Archibald Leach in England, and his desire to dress and act like the "fine gentlemen" he saw in the theater district in London as a small boy shaped his future career.

Assuming we're speaking of a fictional film or book, would we stop the action of the grown man to describe or insert an extensive flashback to a boy enviously looking at the shoes of fine gentleman? No, the more realistic solution is to show a scene in which the character takes a meeting or call while expertly shopping for shoes, or packing for a trip and including many elegant, expensive styles in a specially designed shoe trunk.

Will the audiences "get the fact" that he indulges himself in shoes because he saw elegant footwear as a sign of having "made it" as a youth?

Maybe not. But their curiosity will be aroused, and their awareness heightened. What's with this dude and the shoes?

You can also have backstory come out in the course of dialogue, as long as it's done in a natural way.

In the film *Blood and Sand*, the bullfighter Juan gives a mini-lecture on the subject of making Gazpacho (a peasant dish) at a luxurious dinner table filled with the wealthiest people in Seville. The scene works because it also contrasts Juan's crude manners, favorite foods, and humble background with that of the other guests and his soon-to-be mistress, Dona Sol.

What's also interesting about the scene is that in his own mind, Juan is so consumed with being the "First Man in Spain," in terms of his new celebrity as a bullfighter, he does not see the very real class difference between himself and Dona Sol... and isn't even aware her crowd is making fun of him in its sophisticated, high society way.

From this scene we get a very clear vision that Juan finds it entirely possible that a man born in the lower classes can catapult successfully to nobility. Never does he try to hide his peasant origins, which is part of why he emerges as such a sympathetic character.

Inner Worlds Revealed

Actor Jim Carrey gives many interviews in which he reveals that as a struggling young comic, he used to drive to the top of the Hollywood Hills, look down on the city, and see himself rich and famous. He even wrote a check to himself for five million dollars, such was his confidence that celebrity would be his. No matter that the rest of the world saw he was living in a cheap apartment with his then-wife and baby daughter. In his own mind, he was already famous and wowing the crowds.

Contrast this true-life story (according to Carrey's interview on the E! Entertainment channel) with the fictional character of Bridget Jones.

Just as America learned about the "interior Jim Carrey" from his E! interview, readers and film-goers learned about the fictional Bridget Jones through her diary.

The point is that whether a character is living or fictional, a potential audience grasps at the details of his life to form its own view of that character so strongly the audience feels as if it has enough knowledge to predict how the character would react in specific situations.

Perhaps you have a best friend, relative, or spouse you feel you know like the proverbial "back of your hand." Chances are you can accurately predict what they will do or say in specific situations.

The television show *Trading Spaces* offers a quiz in which contestants must correctly choose the answers their spouses have privately given the host in order to win valuable prizes. Forty years before that show, newlyweds won prizes for correctly guessing their spouses' answers on *The Newlywed Game*.

In both scenarios, the audiences could vicariously join in the fun by virtue of having met the character and making their own assessment.

The audience for your book or film wants to enjoy this same vicarious experience. They want to know enough about your character so they can predict how they will respond to situations that come up in your plot.

As an example, let's use the classic film, *Casablanca* (1942). The plot centers on Rick (Humphrey Bogart), the American proprietor of the most popular bar in Tangiers. At Rick's place, Europeans fleeing war torn Europe wait for their visas to America.

Though we know nothing of Rick when the story opens, we like him. Suddenly, one day in walks Ilsa (played by Ingrid Bergman) and Sam the piano man suddenly plays "their song."

We, the audience, recognize the electrifying moment and though we haven't been told, suspect Rick and Ilsa were former lovers.

Actions speak louder than words.

We don't need volumes of backstory information. We just need to focus on the characters' reactions to one another.

Playing Detective

Much of being an effective writer boils down to your ability to observe the world as if you were a detective. If you watch the popular detective shows on TV you will see that they are constantly making deductions and assumptions about the people they interview. Perhaps like many viewers you almost get an "oh, goody" thrill whenever cops uncover a quirky new twist or development and rush off to question a fresh suspect.

In anticipation of the questioning to come, you are subconsciously wondering:

- ✓ What will the suspect look like (if you haven't yet seen him);
- ✓ How the suspect will react (if you have met him);
- ✓ What excuse will the suspect use to explain his innocence.

In addition, you probably are watching the suspect closely as he answers the detective's questions to see if you can catch him in a lie, or if he looks like he's lying.

Good TV detective story writers and best-selling mystery novelists earn their high pay by their ability to make the audience feel as if it is part of the action and actively solving the crime. Anything less, and the audience feels cheated.

In the same way, refrain from telling the whole story. Give just enough information to let the audience make decisions for itself.

Universal "Good Guy" Characteristics

You already know that your protagonist must be likeable. But what are these qualities, exactly?

Your protagonist does not need to be an angel or as pure as falling snow. In fact, making your protagonist too nice and too perfect renders him unbelievable at best, a toadie at worst.

A good example of a realistic, likeable protagonist is the character Al Pacino played in *Sea of Love*. As the film opens, Pacino's detective character is pouring orange juice for a bunch of guys who think they are there to collect free tickets to a sporting event. Pacino soon reveals both the good news and the bad news: the bad news is that they have all been collected on outstanding warrants and will be bussed to jail. The good news is that they can get vodka shots with their orange juice.

Immediately, we get a sense of Pacino's character as a cop on the "right side" of the law, but with a heart and a sense of humor. His good heart is even more apparent when a dad (presumably guilty of warrant violation) comes by with his young son for the "free tickets" after the others have been arrested. Not wanting to embarrass the father in front of his son, Pacino tells him the tickets are gone and lets him go free.

Nice guy? Yes – at least to the target audience this film is meant to attract.

Take Your Character to a Goal-Setting Workshop

Have you taken a class at an adult education center? Many classes revolve around setting and achieving goals.

Perhaps the best way to learn about your characters and develop their back stories is to take them to a goal-setting workshop.

Even going through the process of developing your character's "SMART goals" on a single sheet of paper will enable you to give your readers a dynamic, three dimensional character with little effort on your part.

As you may have suspected, SMART is an acronym for goals that are:

✓ Specific
✓ Measurable
✓ Attainable
✓ Realistic
✓ Traceable

Let's use the popular classic film *Flashdance* (1983) as an example. The story concerned a pretty girl from a blue collar family, working in a (man's) blue collar job, who really wants to be a dancer many would place between "ballet" and "striptease." She's also in love with a married, well-to-do man, but achieving her dream of being a famed dancer is her immediate goal.

Let's have her attend this workshop and put her SMART goal on paper.

Specific: to be the creator of a new dance between ballet and striptease;
Measurable: getting hired as a "serious dancer" is a measure of success;
Achievable: if she practices and gets a lucky break, sure;
Realistic: She will be a pioneer in the ballet-meets-striptease new dance craze;
Traceable: A steady paycheck and crowd applause will show she's won.

So we have five brief bullet-point sentences that describe the scope of her goal.

Let's look at another example from the classic boxer film, *Rocky* (1976).

Specific: to be a champion;
Measurable: beating the biggest, baddest boxers in the business;
Achievable: others have done it, why not Rocky?
Realistic: practice and will power can do magic;
Traceable: Winning is all that matters.

When you enter a goal-writing workshop, the first thing you are asked is to put your goal on paper. Something in the brain-hand-pen connection makes the goal more concrete than a mere, passable thought.

Exercise: Grab your notebook and right now, put your character's single goal on paper. Now, add his subconscious goal.

By this I mean that characters have both a "story goal" that may read like the "to-do" list you and I write each day as we work toward advancement in our field. In the film *You've Got Mail,* the goal of Meg Ryan's indie bookstore owner would be to have enough inflow to pay her staff and stay in business. Tom Hank's character's goal is to follow his chain store's business plan and put as many indie bookstores out of business as possible.

Meg's character's subconscious goal is to marry someone she loves and have a family. Tom's character's subconscious goal is to find a meaningful relationship.

When the story opens, your characters only know the immediate goals on their "to do" list. This is the framework that guides their actions. But pay close attention to their subconscious goals, and how these hidden goals shape the story.

In *Sea of Love,* Pacino's character was torn between being a good cop and his longing for love and a meaningful relationship. A wrench was thrown into his plans since the object of his desires could be a serial killer, and thus, interfere with his primary goal of being a good cop.

Your characters' goals are the roadmap of your story. Somewhere along the way of living their lives, they switch gears and their priorities change. In *Pretty Woman,* Vivian considered Ed Lewis simply yet another well-paying trick. Her goal was to get the money and continue as before. By story's end, her goals and priorities have changed from that of a hooker on the make to a young lady in search of higher education.

Most characters do not start the story with a wish or goal and see it come true by story's end. The first act of a script or part of a novel must first introduce the characters and what they think to be their objectives which, by the second act or part, turn into something else.

In *Flashdance*, the character's dream was to be a ballet dancer. When that didn't work out, she found success by creating her own dance.

In *Sea of Love*, the character's goal was to find a killer. Instead, he found love... a plot shared in *Basic Instinct*.

The magic of the top grossing films is that the goals characters had at the beginning of the film were transformed by the end.

Back to the Goal Setting Workshop
Okay. Your characters are sitting eagerly in class, waiting for the lesson to begin.

Perhaps like many of us, they have hazy, long-range goals, and they are in class to get in touch with themselves, their desires, and turn their goals into realilty.

In life, you may have noticed that many people are actively pursuing their dreams. These "doers" often get more done the busier they are. Author/publisher Michael Korda published many best-selling books by writing fiction between the hours of four and six am, and then continuing with his day job of running Simon & Schuster afterwards.

Other people have extremely hazy long-range goals that are often overshadowed by immediate needs relating to food, addictive substances, and pleasurable activities. Still others are so worn down by life they feel it's impossible to change their circumstances, so why even try?

Consider that the characters in your goal-setting workshop are a mix of the three.

Have each of your characters write out answers to the following:

1. What are their main objectives?
2. What resources (emotional and financial) do they need to achieve them?
3. List the things that can stop them from achieving their goals.
4. List the people who, consciously or subconsciously, will try to stop them from achieving their goals.
5. List the ways they might sabotage themselves from achieving their goals – and why? (i.e., they secretly fear success).
6. Write a paragraph on how they will feel once they've achieved their goals.

Once your characters fill out their goals, look at the goals as a way to structure the story. Again, your character's goals do not have to be dramatic. They can be as simple as a desire to keep their jobs so they can feed their families, or even stay on unemployment as long as possible so they can continue to watch their favorite soap operas.

Realize that many characters might simply write "I don't have any goals" and look sullenly at the course professor.

One film character who might have done that was Toula, the female lead of the film *My Big Fat Greek Wedding* (2002).

As the story opened, Toula was near middle-age, unmarried, and still living at home. She had accepted her future and, while not happy about it, didn't see a way out. Conceivably, she might have refused to vocalize goals in the class.

When characters write that they don't have any goals on their sheets of paper, it's a signal for you to dig deeper.

It's time for you, posing as a most compassionate teacher, to take the student/character for coffee and gently pry into his or her life.

(Note: be sure to have your notebook ready or computer up and running when you ask the first question, because characters usually give you a "brain dump" and you don't want to miss any juicy nuggets.)

With a teacher's gentle nudging, Toula might slowly admit that she had no goals because her life was a written book. She might have said she was boxed in and couldn't alter her life without hurting her well-meaning parents. She would vent her frustration, cross her arms, and swear she couldn't do anything about her life – least of all make a goal.

In the screenplay, a chance encounter with the man who would be her future fiancé spiked the desire to remake her life — first by losing a bit of weight and looking more presentable and second by getting a job outside the family business, which would generate more potential interaction with men. As it turns out, this is how she meets her fiancé.

So even if you (as author) don't yet understand your characters' goals, sit them down and ask. The amount of information they tell you can write your story for you.

Your Character's Autopsy

It's several decades after your story ends, and your character is on a slab in the Medical Examiner's (M.E.) office in order to determine the exact cause of death. If you've watched or read enough mysteries you know that forensic science is such that the M. E. can learn a great deal about you in this last examination of your life.

M.E.s can tell if (female) characters have had children, if they bite their nails, if they were sexually assaulted in the last minutes of their lives, if they were properly nourished, if they drank or had unhealthy habits, and myriad other details.

Now, while your character is still alive and in his prime, consider pretending he's dead, laying him out on a slab, and calling your favorite fictional forensic scientist to come over and take a look.

When you see your character as a vessel of life experiences, rather than a living human being, you can view the character in a new, unique way. Forensic scientists view their "patients" as a collection of causes and effects. Like archeologists, they view the remains with the objective of imagining not just how they died, but how they lived.

Realize that it might be difficult for you to see your character this way, but that the jolt might also be exactly what you need in order to see your character in a more objective fashion. The exercise should awaken strong, deeply felt feelings about your character you can put to use now, while your character is very much alive.

◆ CHAPTER SUMMARY ◆

In this chapter you learned:

1. Audiences need to be seduced into wanting to learn more about your character.

2. Know as much detailed information about your character as possible.

3. Think of what your character obsessed about as a youth for added richness.

4. Give audiences enough discreet information about your character to empower them to predict how your character will react to specific situations.

5. Learn more about your characters by taking them to a goal-setting workshop.

6. Experience your characters' autopsies to learn more about how they lived.

◆ ASSIGNMENTS ◆

1. Decide how to introduce your characters in ways that will preserve their mystery.

2. Try the exercise "Psychic Doctor" in which you study the scars and distortions on your unconscious characters, intuitively knowing how they got the various scars.

3. Consider what your character thinks about when he's left to his own devices.

4. How does your target audience come to know your character best? Is it through his actions, through conversations with other characters, a development of scenes, a diary?

5. Identify what makes your character likeable.

6. Take your character to a goal-setting workshop and create your own SMART goals for him (Specific, Measurable, Attainable, Realistic, Trackable).

7. Attend your character's autopsy. What did you discover that you hadn't known before?

◆ CHAPTER FIVE ◆

TELEGRAPHING INFORMATION VIA A CHARACTER'S OUTER WORLD

In the previous chapter, we came to know our characters more intimately by glimpsing their "inner worlds" and to a large extent, discovering what makes them tick by discovering key events in their pasts and also, in their distant futures.

This information is important to us, as creators of the characters. Yet most folks judge people, as well as fictional characters, only on the basis of what they wear, what they drive, and where they live. Screenwriter David Tausik and I discussed the fact that in a film, the audience learns a great deal about the character in the first minute by seeing the character and noting what he wears, how he acts, and where he is located.

The film *Fatal Attraction* opens with a slow camera pan of Manhattan, and narrows to a particular upscale apartment building. Inside the window, an audience could see that the apartment was cluttered with a bicycle, toys, and a dog — strongly indicating that this apartment originally may have been owned by a single person who married and procreated, and has now outgrown his space.

This opening shot foreshadows the theme of this film, as the owner of the apartment is conflicted over his desire to be a good husband/father (and move to the suburbs and more space) or retain his single, Manhattan guy status with what turns out to be a near-fatal fling.

A very similar opening pan was used in the Alfred Hitchcock film *Rear Window* (1954) in which the camera enters the apartment of James Stewart's photojournalist character and slowly takes in the pictures, books, and trinkets which tell the story of his life, including award-winning photographs, awards, etc. Before Stewart's character utters a word, we feel as if we know him.

An audience's opinions about the characters, consciously or subconsciously, are drawn from the style of their apartments, their personal items, their clothing, and more.

In the world of film, basic movie-going audiences don't give much thought to the wardrobe designer or the set designer, even though their jobs are crucial to setting the tone of the film. On an E! Entertainment special, the set designer from *Will & Grace* showed a camera crew around the set and explained the decision behind every purchase, saying "Will collects Chinese art" or "Grace really responds to these kinds of paintings." To this set designer, Will and Grace were not characters, they were living people with definitive senses of style.

Your characters deserve the same careful thought and attention when it comes to creating their physical worlds. Put this book down for a moment and if you are at home, look at your living space and try to imagine what assessments viewers would make of you if a camera crew suddenly showed up to film you in your apartment.

As they read your script or book, readers place a high value on succinctly describing your character's "outer world." This does not mean you should write pages of flowery prose describing your character's physical space (particularly for a screenplay). But rather, that you are clear about where they live and the possessions they find important, and showcase this at opportune times.

Your character's physical setting can also foreshadow the dynamics of the plot. The film *Fatal Attraction* opens as the camera pans the glittering city of Manhattan, and then narrows to a small Manhattan apartment in a good, even upscale, neighborhood, entering the space from the window. From the single child's bicycle and strewn-about toys cramping an otherwise neat apartment, it's clear the addition of a growing child and giant dog have cramped what was once the tidy space of a bachelor.

This physical setting literally sets the stage for the action to come. With just the opening visuals, an audience can subliminally understand the plot dynamic, which at its center, concerns a husband and father clinging to the heady Manhattan bachelor days of his youth (both his living space and sexual freedom).

Physical setting is also important in the Hitchcock classic, *Rear Window*. Over the opening credits, the camera pans across an actively awakening neighborhood. Glimpses of a young woman exercising and a couple awakening from sleeping on their balcony make viewers feel like peeping Toms.

Like *Fatal Attraction*, this camera pan of the physical setting strongly ties in with the plot, in which a temporarily handicapped photographer Jeff Jeffries (played by James Stewart), who spends his days looking out the window, becomes convinced he's witnessed a neighbor's murder.

We learn a great deal about Jeffries' character in this extended camera pan. It begins with the wide view of the apartments around the open courtyard, then narrows as it enters, ultimately leaving the neighborhood and pulling into Jeffries' small apartment, focusing on several awards and dramatic war photographs on the wall. From a phone call Jeffries' receives a moment later, we find he's an in-demand war photographer who enjoys putting himself in danger and is bored by present circumstances.

While it's important that you, the writer, take on the role of a set designer and spend serious time imagining how your character's apartment or work space looks, please do not make the mistake of feeling that you have to describe it at length on the opening page.

It's only important that you, the writer, know the possessions important to your character (like the awards and photographs in the above example).

Lengthy description is frowned upon in screenplays and today's novels. Book editors and script readers complain that their eyes glaze over when they read page-length descriptions that clog up the action. What they prefer are "whispers" of taut, highly honed descriptive words.

Using "Things" to Telegraph Your Characters' Lifestyles
In Los Angeles, one's choice of car articulates one's lifestyle. Owners of BMWs broadcast their "brand" to the world. If your characters own BMWs, whatever their income, they are making strong statements. Ditto for Mercedes, Bentleys, Rolls Royces, and Volvos.

How one takes care of one's car speaks volumes. A freshly cleaned, shiny car from the popular designer of the moment says as much about its owner as a dirty, dusty car.

The owners in the first group respect the statements their cars make and, as a group, are so investment oriented and image conscious, they want to maintain their cars' good looks. They are outward oriented in the sense that they know others make judgments of them based on their cars, and they want to give the right impressions.

The owners in the second group either feel satisfied they were able to afford the cars in the first place, or are so self-confident, they don't care what others think of them. The notion that others would judge them on their cars' dust factor does not occur to them. *Can't they see they're BMWs?*

Your key character(s) fit one of these two profiles. Which one is it? *Why?*

Understanding Possessions

A great many Americans are pack rats. They save string and reuse gift paper, buy souvenirs on trips, and keep furniture enshrouded in plastic for the next generation. Others buy expensive couture outfits to wear once before giving them away.

How your character feels about his possessions can be traced back to how his family valued possessions. A person or character who grew up in poverty can just as easily retain his frugal ways, or become extravagant.

If you allow your audience to view your character's home, you must be certain to mention possessions he holds of value. They can be family heirlooms or possessions he's acquired.

While you may or may not allow the audience to see your character's apartment, you must know what it contains, and how it is decorated.

Personal Adornments

Eyeglasses, clothing, shoes, and watches are immediate ways many of us get a bead on new acquaintances. People have their own ways of "reviewing" new acquaintances based on elements they personally find of importance.

If your character is a respected professional in his field and cares what people think of him, you may want to peek inside his closet and shelves of accessories and ask him why he bought specific items in his wardrobe.

Walk down any popular street in your city, be it Rodeo Drive or Main Street USA, and pay close attention to what people are wearing. On Boston's Newbury Street, one can see the following types of people in any given minute:

✓ Professional women dressed in sleek Prada suits and great shoes.
✓ Tourists in T-shirts with corny logos, sneakers, and maps in hand.
✓ Men in suits, many of them with remarkably expensive and well-shined shoes.
✓ European college students dressed "casually" in expensive couture outfits.
✓ Society matrons, fresh from lunching at the Ritz, dressed in Chanel suits.

That morning, the types described above made decisions of what they would wear based on:

✓ How they felt about themselves.
✓ The people who would see them and their expectations.
✓ The way they personally felt it was appropriate to dress.

In the real world, most people are quick to get a feel for how their colleagues or peers dress, and are quick to emulate that style. What about your character? If this is true for him, ask yourself why. Details are what make each of us unique. Consider people you've seen in the last few days whose appearance has made an impression on you.

Recently in New York a dark haired, attractively turned out woman walked down the street with a classic, expensive looking jacket, scarf, and silk blouse. What attracted my eye was that (unlike most women) she wore cufflinks, and the rather loud gold letters were the D&G logo of couture designers Dolce and Gabbana.

What perplexed me was that without the D&G cufflinks, she could have been a conservative (but stylish and elegant) banker. Loud gold cufflinks drew undue attention to her wrists, and while I presume the links to be quite expensive, they somehow cheapened her otherwise expensive and tasteful outfit. In my mind, I was making an assessment of her, and to myself at least, thought that she was the sort who needed the so-called third party endorsement designer logos are said to give.

If this woman was your character, you would want to make sure that with every outfit she wears, there is always one thing a bit "off" – for example, a classic suit with either a shorter skirt or patterned/texture hosiery. Or a wild ornament in her hair that detracts from an otherwise elegant look. Or a wild bag or coat. Just a small detail that would make your audience wonder, "what's wrong with this picture."

When people in reality look too well put together, this can raise red flags, as well. I knew a woman who married a wealthy man. Two days later, she was sauntering down a fashionable street in the exact outfit shown on that month's issue of the celebrated fashion magazine *W* — a wild chartreuse Chanel suit covered by so much jewelry with the familiar, interlocking C's of the Chanel logo, that her outfit seemed inappropriate for casual wear and more appropriate for models on the catwalk, not merely for those attending it.

Interestingly, her wealthy husband failed to understand her free spending ways and they later divorced.

As a writer, the lesson to be learned from the above illustration is that people often use clothing and accessories as a way to project themselves into a fantasy lifestyle that may not even exist in reality.

Often you might see exceptionally wealthy people under-dress, as if to project the aura of just being part of mainstream America. Many Internet gurus, millionaires many times over, take pride in their jean and T-shirt outfits. Some women with teenage daughters of their own continue to buy their own wardrobe from the teen or junior sections of department stores.

And in the film *Erin Brockovich*, Erin (played by Julia Roberts) was characterized by her wild, overtly sexual outfits. In an off-camera interview, Julia Roberts explained that when she put herself into Erin's mind to play the role, she wasn't trying to look sexy. Instead, this is what Erin felt looked nice and acceptable.

Many men wear leather coats (like the ones seen on the younger cast members of HBO's *Sopranos*) that, they may think, make them look the slightest bit dangerous.

Quite a few students from Arab-speaking countries, especially these days, dress like rap stars with baggy pants and the ubiquitous baseball caps, perhaps trying to fit in with mainstream American culture.

When you begin to observe people on the street, you will be surprised by how you immediately make snap judgments about people based on the clothes they wear, and their grooming.

Clothing is a source of expression in our country, and more than ever, there are no rules. Offices have dress codes, but the prevailing standard is "Casual Fridays." In these offices, employees have a choice of three objectives when they dress for work.

The first is that they want to blend in completely with everyone else.

The second is, they want to dress like others, but stand out in some way, perhaps with natural good looks, a great body, a decisive manner, etc.

The third is they want to out-dress others, either because their ego demands it, they are insecure, or they want to use dress as a form of articulating their individuality.

In Los Angeles, it is difficult to see people, especially women, dress up for even the most formal events. Even in suits, most Los Angeles women avoid the de rigueur accessories of scarves and pins of their East Coast sisters. One exception is a woman I'd see working her cell phone day after day in a Brentwood café. Casually dressed, others would swirl around her in the California sunlight, while she was weighted down with so many layers of scarves and jewels she stood out like a creature from another space and time.

When you see someone who takes so many steps to act as a non-conformist, ask yourself "Why?" Like the cover of this book, non-conformist characters are enigmas. It makes us wonder. And getting your audience to wonder about a character is what good writing is all about.

Costume Design and Your Character

It's quite possible you never gave costume design much thought as you write your scripts or novels. The very best costume design is seamless... characters are so believably captured in their eras and social milieus, whatever they wear simply seams natural.

In actuality, designing wardrobe for films that take place in today's world can be as complex as finding costumes for 18th century characters. Wardrobe professionals must figure out what their characters can afford to spend on clothing given their salaries and, given the presumed spending limitation, must mentally "shop" for their characters, taking into consideration popular brands valued by their social groups and their needs (i.e., clothes to wear to work, clothes to wear to the playground with their children).

Clothes are so intrinsically woven into your characters, you might well give serious consideration to their wardrobes now, both in terms of what they can afford and ways they might highlight their individuality.

In the 1960 film, *The Apartment*, a classic film starring a young Jack Lemmon as aspiring executive Bud Baxter and Shirley MacLaine as cute elevator operator Fran Kubelik, Baxter verbalizes he first noticed Fran because of the flower she consistently wore in her uniform. Since Fran didn't make much money, this was the only way she could really distinguish herself.

If your characters are on budgets, think of ways they can show their individuality by dressing with ingenuity rather than cash.

Altered Appearance Can Telegraph Emotional Upheavals

In the film *The Apartment*, Baxter also notices Fran cut her hair. Though Fran doesn't tell Baxter why, a later scene reveals the cut hair and absence of the flower is a result of her frustration that her married executive lover won't marry her.

One of the most universal ways to telegraph an altered appearance and change is through hair.

Throughout history, hair has been one of the key ways that human beings telegraph their status and sexuality. At the height of 17th and 18th century court life in France, young men wore their hair long and pomaded. English court judges still wear powdered wigs that proclaim their status. Even in ancient days, women would spend hours having their hair artfully arranged by servants. Consider how you can use hair to telegraph status or represent the end of a relationship or way of being.

Articulate Character Growth Through Clothing

In the 1938 film *Pygmalion*, the precursor of *My Fair Lady* and *Pretty Woman*, clothing is so intensely used to articulate character growth and development one can clearly follow the film's action with the dialogue turned off. Eliza, the Cockney flower girl, first arrives at Professor Higgins' house in tattered clothes, her hair a mess. By the end of the first act she's been given a bath and appears clean and fresh, nude under her light robe. The next scene depicts her with her hair neat, and in a schoolgirl style dress. As the film progresses, she is seen in slightly more sophisticated daywear before slipping into the fabulous dress bought for her by the Higgins and their friend Colonel Pickering, designed to dazzle (and fool) a high society luncheon crowd into thinking she is a woman of elegance and taste.

Finally, of course, she appears in a fabulous ball gown to pass herself off as a Duchess, which she does successfully.

The film *Pretty Woman* follows a similar method through clothing. When we first meet Vivian, she's a cheaply dressed hooker with a horrid short blonde platinum wig.

Awakening in the freshness of morning, her wig, attitude, and make-up off and her long brown hair spread over the pillow, she looks like any beautiful young girl.

Instead of having Vivian's quest for "appropriate clothing" be a non-event, the writers sagely crafted the scene in which the shop clerks were rude to her, setting the stage for a flurry of new shopping/clothing related scenes that drove the action further and set up Vivian's character – and the characters all around her – more succinctly.

Vivian's breakdown in front of the hotel's general manager (played by Hector Elizondo) and her revelation to him of the rude way she was treated in the Beverly Hills boutique is the pivotal scene that allows Hector's character to take a more central role in the fairy tale story and set in motion the delightful shopping montage (shopping fun set against the energetic *Pretty Woman* theme song) that follows.

Vivian's transformation by clothing is highlighted when her friend Kit (Laura San Giacomo) notices how far she's come with a "you've really cleaned up kid" line and the question of whether she gets to keep the clothes, or not.

Clothing, outside America usually an accurate indicator of social status, takes a pivotal role in the film *Gosford Park*, where both servants and aristocrats harshly judge a new addition to their hunting weekend by the pedestrian state of her clothing.

Clothing and Your Character

If you haven't given thought to how your character dresses, how much he is willing to go into debt for his clothes, or if he conforms to the "norm" of his social network in dress, you must do so now.

Learn to be observant.

See details.

You may see five women wearing jeans and white T-shirts as you walk down the street, but look closely at the jeans. As of this writing there is a "jeans war" going on between the left and right coasts, with women declaring "who they are" by the designer of their jeans. To a Martian from outer space, denim is denim, but the fit, the pre-washed state of the jeans, the low or high rise, and the number of pockets is a keen indicator of their expense and the wearer's sophistication.

If the jeans are low-rise, does the wearer let her navel show? Is it pierced? Does it have jewelry? Is there a tattoo on her stomach?

A very attractive woman I once met wore low rise jeans and a snake tattoo peaking out from them across her stomach. Yet the expensive, tasteful designer jewelry from Cartier in her ears and fingers and wrist, and the fact she was in her forties, contrasted with the tattoo. She didn't seem like a rock n' roll groupie, yet she looked like one. What was up with the tattoo? A secret rebel who frequented biker bars when she wasn't attending prestigious daytime society events?

I asked her about it, and it turns out that the tattoo was to cover a surgical scar. Given the choice between a scar and artful design, she simply chooses the design.

You haven't met this woman, but already, the contrast between her dress, grooming, and the real-life society woman she was made her an interesting character in your mind.

Putting It All Together

Every aspect of a person's appearance offers clues to his emotions, beliefs, and values. Again, we've all been taught never to judge a book by its cover, but we do.

In the course of your daily life, train yourself to become more observant about the people around you, especially strangers. Why strangers? Because it is in our nature as human beings to make "snap judgments" of people we are introduced to, or strike us in some way.

Below you will find a short list of ways we make judgments of people:

✓ Body shape
✓ Facial appearance
✓ Makeup
✓ Hair/grooming
✓ Makeup

What's interesting about this list is that one's judgment of the above elements depends on the norms of the home city.

Manhattan and Hollywood have a narrow definition of what makes up an attractive body. A woman a Southerner would find fit and shapely could very well be called fat on the West coast. Elaborate make-up normal for a Southern woman would be found over-the-top in L. A., a city which favors a lighter hand with the make-up brush and a more natural look.

When you write for films and novels, however, you must venture into the middle ground and tie into mainstream values with regard to appearance.

The film *Working Girl*, starring Melanie Griffith as Tess McGill, is a great example of how writers used popular national stereotypes to propel the story and define characters. In the same "Makeover" theme that defined *Pygmalion* and *Pretty Woman*, Tess's long, teased blonde hair is cut short and her appearance cleaned up before she can successfully pass herself off as an executive. By contrast, her best friend and co-worker, played by Joan Cusack, is still wearing wacky eye shadow in outlandish colors.

The key scene in which Tess's new look and poise are contrasted against Joan's outer-borough "Bridge and Tunnel" appearance and behavior is among the most memorable in the film.

Again, audiences need to see a character transformation, not simply be told this is taking place. Using your character's appearance to "show" change or highlight a popular stereotype based on clothing or makeup is a great way to go.

How to Use Visible Habits to Add Richness and Interest

The best detectives capture criminals by discovering their habits and trapping them at their own game. Each of us has a habitual way of doing things, and whether we know it or not, our habits are visible to all who care to observe.

Right now, let's focus on common, visible habits.

Let us also view the dictionary definition of the word "habit," which is described as "a recurrent, often unconscious pattern of behavior that is acquired through frequent repetition" and "an established disposition of the mind or character."

For example, in this context, cigarette smoking would not necessarily be called a habit. But if an individual or character smoked a cigarette like clockwork after every single meal, smoking a cigarette after every meal would be a habit.

Twirling hair is a common habit for many women with long hair. But you, the writer, must define if your character only twirls her hair when flirting with a man, only when she's alone and thoughtful, or when she's stressed out.

Though you may not be able to articulate it for the screen, realize most people think in a habitual way. We all have a method to our madness. Some of us in managerial positions have learned that it's fruitless to rock the boat by retraining individuals to think like ourselves, we must first understand their habits, and then find innovative ways of incorporating our system into their existing habits of operation.

Relying on habits as clues is what made novelist Agatha Christie's detective novels best-sellers. The detectives weren't school-trained as much as they were keen observers of human nature.

Discovering Patterns

Nearly everyone has a standard way of behaving when faced with familiar circumstances. In fact, the biggest obstacle to personal growth and development is that we become so dependent on our typical patterns of behavior we stop trying new things.

To discover patterns in others and apply them to your characters, begin to play sleuth and keep your notebook with you at all times.

Observe people you encounter in your daily life. Regard them as specimens and look for clues to who they are, who they think they are, who they want others to think they are, etc. This is articulated in our society by dress and grooming.

To discover patterns:

1. Start with striking traits in appearance or behavior.
2. Look for discrepancies between dress (signifying age/class) and behavior.
3. Analyze deviations from the norm.
4. Ask yourself the "why" question:
    – Why is a woman over a certain age dressing like Britney Spears?
    – Why is a man over 40 dressing like a rock star?
    – Why is a high-powered executive taking Casual Fridays to an extreme?
    – Why is your host at lunch carefully reviewing the check?
    – Why are people at the next table speaking loudly, so you can overhear?

Why, why, why? Unless we are Observer types by nature, we rarely question what motivates others.

People are motivated by promise of pleasure or fear of pain, period. Look at your spam e-mail. Chances are you will find a never-ending stream of medication to increase pleasure (Viagra and other substances) or reduce pain. Television advertisers know they must appeal to the pain/pleasure points of our brains, which is why so many TV commercials feature scantily clad women and luscious-looking shots of attractive-looking food.

It's time to start playing sleuth. Keep your notebook with you constantly in an effort to write down "first impressions" of everyone you see. Please note that first impressions do not have to be – nor should they be – politically correct. Rather, they should be "from the gut," so to speak.

In your recorded observations, consider how the traits of people you admire might suit your character. And, by contrast, if you note a person with a characteristic you abhor and feel you personally could correct, consider borrowing this characteristic and giving it to your character.

Understanding "Issues"

Consider what would happen if the world was populated by Barbie and Ken dolls, adjusted for ethnicity. All men would fit the stereotypical image of the romantic/executive hero in that he would be tall, good looking, and dependable. Women would look like Barbie (or actress Pamela Anderson) and share a universal trait of appearing seductive and attractive.

Consider that our world is controlled by genetics while our minds still think "romance novels and Madison Avenue advertising."

Subliminal advertising has infiltrated our culture to the extent that when we first see or meet people, most of us subconsciously measure them against television/media standards of perfection.

Most TV characters are very attractive and fit the cultural norm – ditto for film characters and models in magazines. Many people in the real world, though unable to measure up themselves, are programmed to judge people by media standards.

While giving a talk on presentation skills, I was rather surprised to hear a young, handsome, six-foot-tall class participant state in so many words that he feels men below a certain height inferior. Anorexic women who put their lives at risk by improper eating habits often vocalize disgust with women who are a "normal" weight.

So imagine now what it would be like to be a 5'5" man or slightly overweight woman dealing in today's highly judgmental society. Because others judge us by standards mandated by the media, not their own body shapes, we are "approved" or "disapproved" unconsciously and automatically by how well we match the ideal as highlighted by the media.

Seeing Your Character Through the POV of Other Characters

Psychologist Carl Jung wrote about the Collective Unconscious and Archetypes. While this is a complex philosophy, one can feel comfortable summarizing his theory by saying that he was highly aware of universal symbols.

Marilyn Monroe is a near Universal symbol of female desirability. Every year, other actresses (are you listing, Pamela Anderson?) try to take her place.

For decades, Cary Grant embodied the male ideal – good-looking, sophisticated, and smart. Each year brings sexy, new, young male stars, but Grant and Monroe remain Universal symbols of desire.

Peer pressure and family-rooted prejudices strongly affect how we view strangers. As far as first impressions go, most people note race before noting other qualities. Physical beauty or unusual proportions to the face or body come next.

As we have the most control over attention to grooming and dress, this is the real measure of your character. This is the way your character *chooses to present himself to the outside world*. A woman can carry an old, worn out purse or an expensive, designer evening bag. A man can leave his head bald, buy an ill-fitting wig, or have expensive hair replacement surgery.

Exercise: Right now, consider your character as he appears to you. Then write in your notebook how a few very different people you know would view him, based on their values and the way you know they tend to judge others.

Remember, your character will be judged on the following:

1. What is your character's race? Can his ethnicity have an impact on how he is seen?

2. Are your character's height and weight what others would consider "normal?" If tall, are people always asking him if he plays basketball? If your character is plump or fat, how does he feel about this? Do others make rude comments?

3. Does your character have radically different styles when it comes to dressing for work and dressing on casual days or for fun? High-powered male executives who wear suits during the week and break out the earrings and dress like rock stars during the weekend can indicate they don't quite know who they are. Women who dress provocatively in situations may be making a statement – what is it?

4. Shoes have enormous importance to a wide percentage of the American population. What kind of shoes does your character wear? Why? Does he spend a disproportionate amount of his income on shoes? Does he have favorite designers? Do you think his taste reflects what society deems fashionable?

5. Many people wear jewelry, whether it is symbolic (wedding rings, graduation rings, religious symbols on necklaces) or because it is a great accessory for their outfits. Does your character wear jewelry? Does he choose jewelry so that others will notice and compliment him, or is the jewelry sentimental?

6. Belts are also important in our society and can range from merely functional to designer numbers that showcase our style and invite compliments. Does your character wear a belt? Do others notice?

7. At conventions in America well attended by Europeans, it's often possible to predict who is European by walking 10 feet behind them and observing the fit of his clothing. Can people who have only met your character once recognize him from behind because of some characteristic way of dressing or walking?

8. Grooming of male facial hair is often trend-based and reflects the grooming habits of actors and rock stars, thus overcoming family-based prejudice about goatees and the like. Does your male character have facial hair. If so, is it to emulate a star?

9 What do people think when they first meet your female character? Write down right now how they see her. Do men find her attractive? Does she dress to be attractive to men?

10. How does your female character wear her hair? If long, does it look clean and cared for? Is she wearing long hair to look younger? Does she dress to look younger? Does she avoid telling people her real age? If the answers to the above are yes, why?

11. Judgments are often made on a person's attire not by whether they approve or disapprove of short skirts, but rather, on the occasion. A short skirt on a date is one thing, a noticeably short skirt worn to a conservative job is something else. Does your character dress appropriately for the occasion?

12. Recently, the *New York Times* featured an article on the overtly sexual attire of many entertainment industry executives. Is your character in a so-called "creative profession" (entertainment, advertising) in which she has the opportunity to take liberties with

her business attire. If so, how is the way she dresses for work different than her contemporaries in a more conservative profession?

In 10th century Turkey, citizens were required to wear different colored hats to indicate their status, profession, and religion. Up until the 1940s in America, both men and women wore hats in the city and felt strong pressure to confirm in their style of dress to societal values.

In America today, we dress as we please – yet eyebrows are raised when our appearance seems inappropriate for the situation. Inappropriate can mean being too dressed up for a situation, as well as too dressed down.

Realize that if your character dresses out of context for a given situation others may perceive your character to be:

✓ Seeking attention.
✓ Not understanding basic etiquette.
✓ Self centered, uncaring what others think.
✓ Trying to come across as spontaneous.
✓ Trying to imitate a star with a different body type.
✓ Valuing comfort over fashion.

As you are beginning to discover, there is much more to effective characterization than meets the eye. Knowing in your own mind how your character dresses and lives is your first step to success.

◆ CHAPTER SUMMARY ◆

In this chapter you:

1. Discovered the importance of clearly visualizing where your character lives, what he drives, and how he dresses.

2. Considered how your character would articulate his personality through clothing.

3. Realized that your potential audience is assessing your characters based on the way they are dressed, and the furnishings and neatness of their apartments.

4. Discovered that description can be sandwiched between lines of dialogue in novels to add color and flavor.

5. Found that cars are good ways of indicating status in cities where people drive.

6. Discovered that personal adornments (eyeglasses, clothing, shoes) provide quick ways for your audience to make assessments of your characters.

7. Learned that you can use clothing and changes in body weight or hair to articulate character growth and development.

8. Discovered the importance of noticing how you, yourself, react to people you meet, so you can better understand how your character views other characters, and how he is viewed in return.

◆ ASSIGNMENTS ◆

1. Enlist the help of a friend and sit in a café together with notebooks or paper. Decide on an interesting individual to analyze, and without consulting one another, begin to assess the person in terms of income, profession, and personality style. Discreetly discuss your assessments and note where your views were similar.

2. Deliberately underdress or overdress for an event in a way that would attract notice. How do people look at you? Does anyone make a remark?

3. Go to a store and try on a clothing style you have never tried before. Look at yourself in the mirror and see how drastically different you look from the mental image you usually carry of yourself.

4. Read the personal ads. Try to create a mental picture and personality style of every advertisement you read.

♦ CHAPTER SIX ♦

COLORING DIALOGUE
VIA PERSONALITY TYPE

Now that we have thoroughly immersed ourselves in our characters' inner and outer worlds, it is time to turn our attention to the way they communicate with other characters, as well as the way they verbalize information to the audience.

Developing a keen ear for realistic-sounding dialogue is of key importance. Have you spent time alone in a café, just listening to the way real people speak? Eavesdropping is a time honored tradition among the most effective writers, who realize the value of training their ears to hear new voices, slang, and ways of phrasing words. Each character in your novel or script should speak with a different rhythm and unique choice of words that immediately clues the listener into his personality.

Hollywood gatekeepers (initial screeners) are notoriously demanding when it comes to dialogue. With 109   120 pages to a script, movie dialogue must accomplish a sweep of functions, including:

- ✓ Giving a voice to your character and adding nuances of personality.
- ✓ Cluing the audience into his geographical and socio-economic origins.
- ✓ Revealing his closely hidden feelings about characters he interacts with.
- ✓ Furthering the plot action of the story.

For their first drafts, many writers are so preoccupied with getting the story down on paper they don't take the time to really focus on their characters' dialogue and think about how, and why, the characters use the phrases and tones that they do. If anything, first draft dialogue looks formal, correct, and entirely stilted to the ear.

In the real world, people, especially in casual conversations, speak in a pattern of stops and starts.

Spoken Motivation

When people and characters decide to take action, they must have motivation to take that action. How you express your desire through your tone of voice is more revealing than the words themselves.

Sales professionals shoot to the top of their field by their ability to instantly gage people and use the right words and right tone to appeal to clients. Socialites can use tone, inflection, eye contact, and gestures to "cut" a social aspirant, crown a new socialite sycophant, or make a statement about their wit via dialogue.

In screenplays, your mastery of dialogue on the opening pages signals to the gatekeeper your script has promise and motivates him to keep reading. This initial read is more of a fast, 15-minute skim in which the dialogue is scanned and expected to tell the story and personality of the characters. If the gatekeeper finds this dialogue scan rewarding, he will set the script aside for in-depth analysis.

Therefore, your dialogue must sing.

Andy Warhol was the first to express the concept of 15 minutes as a key unit of time. Though Warhol applied this concept to fame, learning specialists have determined that an audience will give a speaker/teacher/presenter 15 minutes of attention before a new stimulus is needed to give new focus on the central point. For example, speakers might lecture for 15 minutes, then turn to an interactive exercise for another 15 minutes which reinforces what listeners have learned.

In that 15-minute dialogue scan, the gatekeeper must:

- ✓ Get a strong sense of the protagonist's personality.
- ✓ Get a strong sense of what the story is about.
- ✓ Get a strong sense of obstacles the hero must overcome.
- ✓ Get a strong sense of the minor characters.
- ✓ Get a sense of the protagonist's love interest (if there is one).
- ✓ Get a sense of each character's speech patterns.

Effective dialogue allows the speaker to express personality in addition to making a statement that furthers the plot. This is true of both screenplays and novels.

The 1950 film *All About Eve* starring Bette Davis is an excellent film to view for students of movie dialogue. Bette Davis and the rest of the cast offered up lines of dialogue so expertly written, honed, and spoken that to this very day, witty verbal snippets from the film are quoted in casual conversation, especially in the theatrical gay community.

One of Davis's most memorable bits of dialogue is the line "Buckle up, it's going to be a bumpy night" which follows a scene in which she jealously learns her lover is paying undue attention to her assistant, Eve Harrington, during a party.

Davis's dialogue was such a suburb blend of her own personality, the personality of the character, and the skilled craft of screenwriter

Joseph L. Mankiewicz, every line is perfection. But nearly equal to Davis's dialogue is the sardonic, droll banter of the sophisticated and cruel social columnist character of Addison DeWitt (played by George Sanders), whose voice and personality is described in the film as "snide and vicious."

Every line DeWitt utters expresses his personality, in addition to revealing story information. Moreover, DeWitt uses dialogue as a chess player uses his pieces in that he rarely speaks without looking at the "social board" and making an appropriate move.

Creating Dialogue Through Personality Type

Now we will focus on the four main personality types explained in the More-Personality system. As you will recall, those styles include the Mover, Energizer, Observer, and Relater.

Once again, here are their characteristics:

Mover – brash, "Type A" personality, result driven, fast moving & thinking;
Observer – factual, observant, often insecure, focused on detail, aloof;
Relater – encourages & motivates others, service-oriented, likes human contact.
Energizer – storyteller, confident, ambitious, likeable, charming, quick thinking;

Each of these styles has a specific way of distributing verbal information.

The Mover Character

A Mover will be the most specific and direct in his messages. In the above-mentioned film, *All About Eve*, it was the lead character of Margo Channing, played by Bette Davis, who was the true mover. Margo always explicitly said exactly what she meant, and like all true Movers, didn't have the time to engage in idle chit chat. This turned out to be her downfall when she arrived so late for a reading that her understudy, Eve Harrington (played by Anne Baxter), won the role.

The Mover personality fancies that the world runs like the proverbial Swiss Train, always on time and reliable to the core. Operating in a world characterized by the laws of cause and effect, the Mover expects that if he does or says "x" everyone will carry out his orders. Filled with an overwhelming sense of self-importance and accustomed to people bowing and scraping in his wake, the Mover would never take the time to be artfully manipulative with his words (a characteristic of the Energizer) or verify his facts, as would the Relater.

One can see evidence of the Mover personality style evidence through Davis's character of Margo Channing in many scenes. One of the first occurs when her friend Karen Richards (played by Celeste Holme) first ushers the character of Eve Harrington into the dressing room. At this early point in the film, Eve is impersonating a shy, down on her luck admirer.

In true Mover style, Channing is forthright in dialogue and tells her assistant to give Eve the "heave ho" and throw her out.

Yet Karen Richards, a Relater, pleads with Margo to let her stay, a pivotal scene in the film that paves the path for Margo's downfall.

In the skillful hands of screenwriter Joseph L. Mankiewicz, this scene was believable because he so successfully created Margo Channing as a sucker for flattery and a dramatic sob story. But if you have created a Mover character, do not expect him to acquiesce to requests so easily. And if he does, be aware that it will be the most pivotal scene in your book or film script.

Tips on Crafting Mover Dialogue

Mover dialogue is direct and to the point. Think "bullet points" and not complete sentences. When Movers are asked a polite "How are you" they commonly give "action words" as a reply, such as "moving along."

When you think of a Mover in your mind, you may try visualizing the color red, the color of action and animal passion.

In your notebook, write down as many questions as you can gather that epitomize daily conversation, such as:

- ✓ How are you?
- ✓ What's new?
- ✓ What's up?
- ✓ How are things going?
- ✓ How is your family/spouse/child?
- ✓ How's the project going?
- ✓ How's business?

Now, think of the color red and a no-nonsense, very busy person and fill in the response.

A Mover would rarely say "okay."

A Mover would rarely say "great."

If forced to give a short answer, a Mover would use an action phrase, such as "moving along!" Or, when inquiring about another project, the Mover might say: "Great! Now let's get back to issue A. Have you heard from your source?"

Movers do not speak to be charming. They don't have time to engage in idle chit chat – not with their meters ticking. Questions are blunt and direct. Replies to questions manifest in grunts, one-word replies, or questions in return. Meaningful conversations are oxymorons.

When Movers do speak, they often are unaware of the derogatory, cutting nature of their words. Often enough, their intention is not to be demeaning. Given their choice, they do not necessarily wish to belittle people. Yet they swiftly get this reputation.

Movers are on a mission, and nothing – especially the niceties of polite conversation – can deflect them from their goals. Films usually "soften" a basic Mover by giving him strong Energizer characteristics, since the classic Mover might be perceived as too abrupt, especially in conversation. People and audiences respond to warm, red-blooded characters with charm and compassion for others, qualities the action-obsessed Mover character often lacks.

The closest example of a solid Mover character was played by Michael Douglas in the film *Wall Street*. While a strong Mover, the character also had equally strong Energizing qualities, notably in his ability to persuade others to subscribe to his beliefs.

Bette Davis is a Mover in *All About Eve*, and convincingly comes across as cold blooded and cold hearted. Her only "weakness" is for her handsome playwright lover, and in terms of her dialogue, it's only to him that she uses tender, empathic words. In one key scene, she's such a cold-hearted Mover she finds it impossible to even pronounce the words "I love you" on a long-distance telephone call, calling it "kid stuff."

Exercises:
Think of your Mover character. Open your notebook (or a computer diary) and ask your Mover these questions:

- ✓ Tell me about the movie you saw last night?
- ✓ What did you think of that hot new restaurant?
- ✓ What did you think of the gown Jennifer Lopez wore on the Academy Awards?

How would they answer the questions? Quickly and to the point. Their patience has a limit, but they don't have to be universally terse. Even if they give complete sentences to employees, it doesn't mean they'd show the same courtesy to clerks at department stores.

Movers, as a group, tend to compartmentalize people.

Showing your Mover extend more courtesy to some people and less to others via the terseness of his dialogue paints a more vivid, and realistic picture of your Mover. This can be a good thing if your Mover is unsympathetic. But this quality will render him less likeable as a protagonist.

In the film *You've Got Mail*, Tom Hanks played a Mover to a large extent, but because he had to be sympathetic, the screenwriters toned down his harsher Mover qualities and gave him more people skills. Instead of being impatient with people verbally, his negative Mover characteristics come out in how rude he is to others. To show his selfish nature, at a party Hanks' character is shown scooping all the caviar decoration off a buffet entrée, echoing the real-life way he scoops the cream from little bookstores to add to his bookstore empire.

Another tactic used to soften Hanks' natural Mover characteristics is a scene with his own father, a Mover more insensitive than himself.

As you write your Mover's character, in addition to visualizing the color red, visualize a strong sense of movement. A Mover's words are movement oriented. For example, if a Mover were listening to you in a meeting, he might say things such as:

✓ Let's cut to the chase....
✓ What's the bottom line?

✓ How do you propose to go from A – Z?
✓ Can we zip forward to the next issue?
✓ Let's skip over this section....
✓ Moving right along....

To summarize, think carefully about how strong you want to make your Mover, especially if the Mover is the protagonist.

The Energizer Character

Let us turn our attention to the Energizer style. Preachers are good examples of Energizers. Watch just an hour of religious services on Sunday morning television and you will see a preacher or minister whip his congregation into shape by the force and fire of his words. Energizers use the power and manipulated tone of their words to change opinions, minds, and emotions.

In *All About Eve,* this style is best reflected in the characters of Eve Harrington and Addison DeWitt.

As you may have discovered in the previous chapter, often it is difficult to tell the difference between a Mover and an Energizer. In fact, many Energizers find that when they take the MORE Personality™ Quiz they have strong Mover scores. The key difference between the Mover and Energizer style is that Movers do not play games. When they want something done, they command it. Energizers are more like cats, using charm to manifest their desires from others. And like cats, when they are crossed, they take delight in toying with their victim.

The character of Addison DeWitt, expressed through dialogue, epitomizes the Energizer style. Like all Energizers, he is fascinating to watch in action. He is also a born storyteller, a quality that comes out in casual dialogue, as well as the tone and structure of his written columns.

DeWitt's calculating mind makes it easy for him to unleash his sharp tongue quickly when victims least expect it. His verbal retorts are crafted for his own amusement, and for the amusement of those around him, such as is demonstrated in the staircase scene at the end of the party, in which the group literally listens at his feet. DeWitt enjoys the admiration of a crowd – it inspires him, as it does all Energizers who need an audience to reflect their glory.

Eve Harrington is also an Energizer. When you see the film, notice how similar her verbal personality is to DeWitt in that she always seems to be speaking from the stage (though less imposingly than Margo). Like DeWitt, Eve is a remarkable storyteller. In fact, it is her skill with storytelling (telling lies, actually) with such heart-wrenching drama that won her the opportunity to work as Margo Channing's maid. Eve thrives on admiration from the crowd, and would take any step necessary to achieve her desire.

Energizers frequently speak as if they are, in fact, telling stories. They rarely utter words simply to make statements. They want to convey emotions in their statements, and in addition, want to "push forward their pawns" as if playing a game of verbal chess.

Before your Energizer opens his mouth, imagine a stereotypical English chap prefacing his statement with "I say."

The stress is on the word "I." Translated, imagine your Energizer character clearing his voice, clapping his hands, and virtually saying "Listen up, folks, I'm going to make a statement and it's going to be a dazzler."

Consciously or subconsciously, Energizers often speak loud enough to be overheard, as if they hope other people will hear their words and be intrigued by their brilliance. You can see this quite clearly in DeWitt's character in *All About Eve*. He considered every syllable he uttered a jewel.

Now consider how your Energizer would answer the same questions asked of your Mover. Ask a Mover to tell you about a movie and you are likely to be greeted with "it was okay." Ask the same question of an Energizer and you would know exactly what made it so terrific, or so dreadful, with a million droll details thrown in for good measure. Ask the Energizer his thoughts about a restaurant, and he'd discuss the colorful scene, as well as the food. Your Energizer will feel quite comfortable embellishing the truth to make the story juicier and livelier.

Kate Hudson played an Energizer in the film *Almost Famous*. As the character Penny Lane, she attracted the camera like a magnet in virtually every scene. When she spoke, her eyes would first light up with excitement as if to say, "this is my moment to shine!"

In contrast to the acerbic Addison DeWitt of *All About Eve*, Penny Lane's words, verbatim, were far from brilliant. An Energizer doesn't necessarily speak to convey important information. Rather, words are their tools for attracting attention and charming people, so the focus is on how words are spoken, rather than their specific content.

Unlike the Mover, it's difficult to mark the Energizer with a given color. Rather, they seem best characterized by a compelling scent that teases the senses and intrigues all who meet them.

Energizers' dialogue is best characterized by their ability to paint an intoxicatingly vivid picture of a desirable future event, and to spellbind others listening to their stories like toddlers listening to a favorite fairy tale.

Energizers know how to persuade others to their points of view through the power of contrast.

Regardless of their job descriptions, all Energizers are sales people at heart – even if some find the concept of selling anything repellant. Their "win factor" is wrapped up in having people recognize them as individuals of value. Even for Energizers in sales fields, their glory is not in a dollar amount, but in using enough charm and powers of persuasion to make the deal.

The Energizer character of Penny Lane was all about seduction, in charming her way to getting exactly what she wanted. Ditto for the Energizer characters of Eve Harrington and Addison DeWitt, though his perfumed, parlor-snake persona was venomous, in addition to seductive.

Energizers measure their success by their ability to seduce and control. If Movers use words with an action theme, then Energizers use highly charged visualization words such as "what would happen if" or "can you believe that" or "imagine if."

Energizers also use words that involve the five senses. They want whomever they are speaking with to see the image conveyed by their words, smell the enticing fragrance of whatever they are describing, hear its wonderful sound, and virtually touch it.

Energizers use their words to put their listeners in an exciting new state. When your Energizers speak, take a moment to project how they would add visualization words to what they want to say.

The Observer

As you know from previous chapters, Observers are characters who seek out the truth, even though they risk their lives to do so. One of the most beloved Observer characters in the last half century is Jake Gittes of the Academy Award-winning film *Chinatown*.

It's good to automatically think of an Observer character as a detective, even if he's actually an attorney or even a merchant. Observers – like Jake Gittes – are curious about the world around them and supremely confident in their ability to get to the bottom of any mystery.

When you screen *Chinatown*, you might notice reasons why Gittes risked his life, whereas your character wouldn't. First and above all, Gittes was single and had no dependents. If your Observer character supports a family, odds are he wouldn't get himself so involved.

Second, Gittes was sexually intrigued by the female lead played by Faye Dunaway. Sexual allure has a long history of having men risk their lives to earn favor.

In the film *The Untouchables* (1987), Kevin Costner starred as Elliot Ness, a government agent obsessed with capturing Al Capone. Even though continuing to work on the case put the life of Ness, as well as the lives of his wife and child in jeopardy, he packed his family off to safety and continued his hunt for the criminal. This stubborn insistence in carrying out the mission is the mark of a true Observer.

Movers will pursue their goals diligently, but plain common sense (such as asking who will provide for their families should they be killed in their missions) is usually enough to help them see the light of day. Observers simply can't rest until they finish the job.

Details preoccupy the life of an Observer. They lay awake at night and think about the events of the day, piecing them all together. Professionally, Observers do well as detectives, attorneys, engineers, scientists, researchers, and other fields in which details play a key component.

Mentally, many people make a connection between the Observer style and a "geek" – but this isn't necessarily true. Observers are also artists, fashion designers, make-up artists, and involved in other glamour fields. Andy Warhol was an Observer.

When an Observer speaks – which is rarely to hear the glory of his own voice – it is usually to ask a question that will elicit more information on the subject of his desires.

Chinatown's Jake Gittes typifies the Observer style in that when he does open his mouth, it's to ask a question related to his objective. In contrast to the Energizer, the Observer feels no need to use flowery language or butter his subject up before he asks the question.

Like the Mover, he is direct when asking questions, but has infinitely more patience than the Mover. Movers usually want "bullet point" answers. Observers prefer to ask open-ended questions so that others will reveal enough information for the Observer to pick up on a new thread and ask yet more questions.

An Observer is always walking around, wondering about the "why" of things. In *Chinatown*, one of Gittes's first enigmas was wondering why the dead water executive Hollace was found with saltwater in his lungs if he supposedly drowned in a reservoir.

Even when an Observer is in love, it doesn't put an end to the questioning. Gittes quizzed love interest Evelyn Cross Mulwray even when they were in bed together, and hit her with questions and physical violence when he suspected she was playing him for a fool (such as the scene in which he slaps her around when she insists the girl she's harboring is both her daughter and her sister).

Before you write dialogue for your Observer, be certain that the dialogue is either in question form, or is designed to turn the conversation to a subject that will satisfy his curiosity. Realize, as well, that Observers tend to be quiet and do not speak unless there is a strong reason for it. Andy Warhol rarely spoke unless it was to give a directive to his staff or pronounce an idea or piece of art fabulous.

When Observers do make statements, they rarely open their mouths unless they can "prove" whatever it is they have to say. When an Observer is asked to give a speech, he will research his speech and verify points he wishes to make. Often he will go overboard on the PowerPoint, filling the slides with various charts and graphs.

One of the most irritating verbal habits of Observers is their insistence that they are right. The subject can be related to sports or restaurants, but if someone makes a statement they feel is incorrect, they have absolutely no qualms about correcting them, even if the correction results in an altercation or even violence.

Observers tend to use words that are quantifiable. If they are giving a recipe, they will be quite exact in terms of measurements. If you are creating an Observer character that will be funny, marking the character by his exaggerated correctness can be the stuff of humor.

Quotations are often used by Observers in the course of casual conversation, as if even their personal opinions need to be referenced. As they have a keen eye for detail and tend to memorize facts and quotes easily, quotations roll naturally off their tongue.

The Relater
Relaters are most often secondary characters because they lack the strong emotional drive of the other personality types. Actress Diane Keaton played the role of the Relater in virtually each of

her film roles, especially *Father of the Bride*, *The First Wives Club*, and *The Godfather*.

Yet Keaton only played one side of the Relater, which is the kind, motherly, nurturing side. Ironically, of all the four personality styles, the Relater is most complex.

With a Relater, what you see is not necessarily what you get. On the surface they often appear all sweetness and light, helpful and supportive. Yet beneath their placid, smiling exteriors lies a creature hungry for love and appreciation, needy and clingy at best, psychotic and violent at worst.

In his dialogue, the Relater uses words designed to put people at ease, make them feel comfortable, and make them feel good about themselves. Relaters often give compliments, even when they are not deserved, because by giving compliments they feel they are making the other person like them more.

Relaters also engage in gossip, again as a way of making other people feel they are adding value to the conversation by giving them new, juicy information.

Like Energizers, Relaters are good storytellers and often exaggerate details. They love to talk, love to converse, and are addicted to the phone.

Energizers like to talk because they want others to approve of either the content of their words, or their dramatic way with words. They love the spotlight. By contrast, Relaters love to talk because when they are actively speaking, they feel as if they are needed.

What drives Relaters in virtually every situation is their near obsessive desire to be loved and needed. They become familiar with strangers very quickly, often take liberties by shortening the names of friends and colleagues without permission, and love to pry into the personal life of friends and strangers alike.

When shaping dialogue for your Relater character, remind yourself that 90% of the time he is in an emotionally needy state. Words are a tool he uses to have others give him praise, express appreciation, and otherwise show they value him – hence the effusive compliments and colorful gossip always emanating from his lips.

If you have Relater characters in mind for your novel or screenplay, realize they are often used as functionaries in the Diane Keaton sense – the stereotypical nurturing wife and mother, the good friend, the supportive relation, etc.

However, it is possible to create Relaters with depth (and supporting actor or actress potential) by crafting their characters so that the audience can see growth and change as the story develops. A good example of this type is the character Renée Zellweger played in the film *Jerry Maguire*. While the camera never portrayed her as a gossip, a snoop, or a sycophant, she was an idealized Relater in that she supported her man (without making him jump through the hoops) in exchange for being clear that she expected to be loved and respected in return.

Just as an Energizer speaks with words using the five senses, the Relater speaks in words that evoke emotion. Whereas the Mover is focused on a clear objective, the Energizer's goal is to showcase himself and his abilities, the Observer wants to get to the root of the issue, and the Relater is wrapped up in feeling safe, secure, and loved. The Relater's emotional center is a family or group of friends, and this emotional center colors his dialogue.

Understanding Dialogue

When you receive an e-mail from a friend, chances are you don't even need to read the "from" line to know who sent it. Of all forms of writing, e-mail reads as if the person is speaking to you, not writing to you.

Your friends and acquaintances each have their own rhythms of speaking, favorite words and expressions, and ways of phrasing that are unique.

Consider that your characters have their own way of speaking, as well. Mastering the art of effective dialogue is crucial in terms of getting your screenplay and novel sold. As you have previously read, the reason isn't solely because many agents, editors, producers, and readers "skim for dialogue" but also because in the fictional world, dialogue defines your characters.

By this stage in your writing career, you have received feedback on your work. Chances are mentors, teachers, and friends have commented on your skill with story, characters, and dialogue.

Can you remember what feedback you got on your dialogue? If you've been praised that it's the best part of your writing, congratulations. Keep up the good work. If you've been gently told that this area needs improvement, be confident that with applied effort, you can master this skill.

As you learned, Ray Bradbury first received his characters as voices.

Voices have personality.

In the dark days before television, families would gather around a radio for nightly entertainment. The characters they heard over the airwaves were vibrant and colorful, and came to life solely in dialogue.

Radio narration might set up situations, but it was the interplay between the voices that told the story.

Audiences determined which characters were speaking by the tone and cadence of the characters' voices, as well as familiar words or slang the characters would use.

Let's consider novels. Because novels are read and readers must give a voice to each character, the author must work double duty to ensure that each character speaks like a unique being and in his or her own voice.

If all the characters used the same slang and had the same rhythm and structure to their voices, the audience might get confused.

Both novelists and screenwriters should write dialogue as if the character's name would never be mentioned and assume that the audience will figure out who's speaking.

Dialogue Must Have Purpose

Our first attempts at writing dialogue may have been clumsy ones. Reasons vary, but it could be because we didn't yet understand the character's voice, didn't have a good sense of his personality, hadn't figured out what made him tick, or intuitively used dialogue as a method of explaining information to the audience or furthering the plot.

You might ask... "Isn't dialogue used to explain information?"

Of course. But at the same time dialogue explains information, it must also reveal backstory and character. Otherwise, it sounds stilted, as if the author or screenwriter assumes his audience is so dimwitted he must explain the story points and character interactions.

At the end of many Sherlock Holmes movies the film closes with Sherlock saying, "So you see my dear Watson…" and then retelling and explaining everything the audience had seen to that point. While this might work in a Sherlock Holmes film because the audience has come to expect it and it is a tradition of the literary and film series, avoid this technique in your own work.

Included in the DVD of the Academy Award-winning film for *Gosford Park* (2001 Best Original Screenplay, 2001 Best Director) is a commentary by director Robert Altman. In this commentary, Altman vocalizes many intriguing statements about characterization and dialogue.

If you have not seen the film, it is a murder mystery set in an elegant English country estate. Before the hunting weekend is over, the master of the house is murdered – twice. The police are baffled but the all-seeing, all-hearing servants know that almost everyone had a motive.

In the commentary, Altman admits that many people walk out of the film confused about the culprit(s), a possible motive, and states that few people "get it" the first time they see the film. Dialogue is left deliberately obscure instead of loaded with clues that would have aided audience understanding. Upon seeing the film a second time, an audience hears clues in dialogue that went unnoticed before, and from more carefully observing the characters, sees things it hadn't.

What's valuable about Altman's approach to filmmaking is that his focus is on articulating characterization exclusively through dialogue. For a variety of reasons, he assigned the actors to research their own characters (aristocratic characters would read about the daily lives and customs of real life aristocrats, servant characters would research the lives of real servants), and from this research, give themselves airs, mannerisms, and ways of speaking dialogue that would imbue the story with realism.

In other words, even though the film was technically a murder mystery, the focus of the film was on characterization. Dialogue – if one listened carefully – did provide *whodunit* clues, but the real purpose of the dialogue was to articulate character.

In your story, each of your characters has a goal and objective. Your character also has a history – events that shaped him and brought him to where he is when the story begins. Your character also has a personality, a vocal inflection, and a way of arranging his words that make him unique.

All of the above elements come together in dialogue.

Each line of dialogue needs to accomplish one or more of the following:

- ✓ Give insight into the personality of the character speaking.
- ✓ Give the audience backstory on an issue central to the plot.
- ✓ Heighten tension through conflict.
- ✓ Relieve tension through comedy.
- ✓ Telegraph relationships between characters by how they address one another.
- ✓ Move the story along at a brisk pace.

Conveying Backstory Through Dialogue

"Backstory" is a term that refers to what happened in the characters' lives before the story began. While you, the creator of the characters, need to know their pasts, the audience only needs to know the part of the past that is important for understanding the characters and/or the story being presented. Amateur scripts are filled with scenes in which a character sits another character down and tells the story of his life.

Wrong move.

Space is short, and if a past incident must be revealed, it should be done so in the most succinct manner possible.

In *Pretty Woman*, Vivian is set up as a hooker with a heart of gold. In fact, she's so endearing an audience may wonder why she became a hooker in the first place. Instead of having a long, drawn out scene in which Vivian explains herself, the authors simply have her make a vague allusion to possible sexual abuse at home, and continue on with the story. The scene also serves another purpose, which is to underscore how close and intimate Vivian and Edward become in the course of the week they've spent together.

Effective dialogue reveals layers of personality, which is especially important when we're being introduced to a character we know little about.

In the first act flirtation scene of *Fatal Attraction*, characters Alex Forrest and Dan Gallagher have dinner at a bar and talk about themselves. At a certain point, Alex reels in for the kill. She does this rather ingeniously by playing hard to get, and inferring that even if Dan wanted to take her out, she wasn't sure she'd accept. This brings out the competitive spirit in Dan, and the tide of the conversation turns. Now it's Dan who actively pursues Alex. As a result, they go off together and make mad passionate love. Just from this brief snippet of conversation, the audience gets a very vivid sense of their personalities.

The most straightforward element of dialogue is moving the story from point A to point B. It's important that the audience get a sense of what the story's about as quickly as possible. In addition, the author needs to imbue every line of dialogue with subtext that reveals the speaker's attitude, personality, or emotional layer.

The film *Gosford Park* features a character who plays a butler, but in actuality is a Hollywood actor using the hunting weekend invitation as a way to prepare for a role. The story is written so that no one – neither the audience, the aristocrats, nor the servants suspect this. Yet when the trick is revealed, suddenly it all makes sense.

Why?

At the point of revelation, our minds turn back to small bits of dialogue we heard that didn't seem important at the time, but suddenly make sense.

For example, the butler had a Scottish accent, but one of the Scottish maids says she never heard the accent in any region she's been in.

Throughout the film, aristocrats, servants, and the audience alike are keenly aware of the estranged relationship between the two top employees of the house, the cook and the head housekeeper. Friction characterizes their every interaction together, and in dialogue they struggle to be civil with one another. At story's end, we discover they are sisters and that events in their youth resulted in their current silent feud, as well as tie in with the murder mystery theme.

The revelation comes as a surprise, because while none of this was "told" in backstory, suddenly it makes sense.

You would do well to approach backstory in this way, giving just enough information for your audience to understand each character and speculate on what his past may have been, without typing it out verbatim in black and white.

Perhaps you have seen films with scenes in which the lead character explains his past to a new lover or friend. This took place in *Pretty Woman*, as Vivian explained to Ed why she became a hooker, after lovemaking. Saccharin, yes, but the scene was mercifully short and given the options, perhaps the least time-consuming way to reveal story information. Ed also reveals his difficulties with his father to Vivian in a later scene as they relax under a tree.

Instead of resorting to such stilted dialogue, try to find new ways of revealing backstory. A character can make a sarcastic reference to an object given him by a former lover or estranged family member, for example, revealing just enough story information to "suggest" an unhappy relationship or home life, rather than lay it out slowly in agonizing detail.

Remember – your audience does not care about your protagonist's past. It cares only about your protagonist. If your story requires information about the protagonist's tortured or glorious past life, try to work it in as a glib one liner, albeit one filled with irony or pain.

Bringing the audience up to date on everything that transpired before the story opened stalls the story action. It's like meeting an attractive stranger who opens his mouth to speak… but it's all about the way his parents preferred his older brother or how he never made the high school football team. More information than we needed, or wanted, to know.

Many people are frustrated by their pasts. They feel they did not get the respect or opportunities they deserved. They feel slighted and it still smarts, 10, 20, or 30 years later.

This frustration can actually be the source that propelled them to success.

As creator of your story, you may feel it is important that the audience knows your character's backstory from the first page. Remember that your protagonist's feelings may be universal, and that other people can relate to his frustration without having to be told "the whole story."

The secret of best-selling novelists and screenwriters is using universal experiences to make the audience identify with the protagonist.

For example, the commercial hit film *You've Got Mail* features Tom Hanks as the bookstore chain czar, Joe Fox. In a scene near the third act, Fox has a heart-to-heart talk with his dad, and we learn that Joe grew up with a man who had little respect for family (divorcing his mother, marrying a younger woman), which is meant to explain his mentality.

Look to the world around you in your effort to articulate backstory through dialogue. Ask yourself these questions.

- ✓ Have you figured your colleague's background? How?
- ✓ Has your coworker ever revealed personal information? Why? What are your assumptions?
- ✓ Have you speculated on the family life your boss experienced when growing up? What were your speculations?
- ✓ Do you have friends or acquaintances who are secretive about their pasts? Why do you think this is so?
- ✓ During your education, have you had a teacher or instructor who intrigued you? Why is it?

How to Create Dialogue Tags to Differentiate Characters

Viewers and readers form impressions of your characters based on the things they say, and how they say them. In the classic film *Saturday Night Fever* (1977), John Travolta's character, Tony, was a painter who lived to dance and enjoy the women who came along with nightclub celebrity. The girl he tries to impress, Karen Gorney, is actively trying to better herself – starting with improving her speech.

Regional accents can cause people to be stereotyped and dismissed. When we see characters such as *Saturday Night Fever's* Karen or *Pygmalion's* Eliza taking steps to lose their regional accents, we are motivated to root them on as characters for the simple reason that they are proactively trying to improve their stations.

At the same time we, as an audience, have formed our own stereotypes about accents, so unless there's a key story reason why your character needs to have an accent, you are best served leaving it out of the story.

Instead, look for vocal inflections in the world around you and jot them down in your diary to use on your characters. The inflection that characterizes "Valley Girl Speak" is old news, especially for teens who all seem to speak that way, even if they live in New Jersey. But a 50-year-old woman who uses terms like "oh, my God!" and speaks in this affected manner could be interesting.

In order to make her patois believable, you would have to figure out why a middle-aged woman is compelled to speak like a teen-age girl. You can't just give her this vocal inflection to add character depth – she must speak this way for a reason that's important in your story.

By the same token, if you have a 20-year-old male character who purposefully speaks with the measured words of a professor, ask yourself why. Is he trying to prove something? Is he trying to make up for the fact his father is a janitor? Again, characters need reasons for the way they speak.

The dialogue on the hit TV show *Will & Grace* is clever, funny, and hip. The show's sophisticated fans, especially in big cities and in the gay community, can relate to the way the characters speak. Even so, you will note that Will doesn't speak like Jack, and Karen doesn't speak like Grace. Each of these characters exists in the same chic urban settings yet each has a dynamically different way of speaking.

Karen's tag is that she speaks with a whine, reflecting her selfish, spoiled nature. Ditto for Jack, whose every line expresses a need for love and admiration – or a snide, stinging retort. Both Will and Grace speak like educated, sensible adults, yet each has his or her own particular way of putting words together, expressing problems, etc.

Exercise: So, how do you create unique dialogue for your characters? The answer is two-fold. First, go out into the world. Take your notebook and hang out in a busy Starbucks or open-air café. Listen to how people speak.

When you find someone with an interesting voice, eavesdrop. See how much you can guess about your characters through their dialogue. Ask yourself:

- ✓ Are they educated? How can you tell?
- ✓ Are they married? Why do you think so?
- ✓ Do you like them? Would you want them as friends? Why?

✓ What do you think they do for a living?
✓ If they had cars, what would they drive?
✓ If they had homes, where would they live?

While you won't be able to prove your thoughts are correct, you have taken the first step in understanding the power of deciphering character through dialogue.

How to "Hear" Your Characters' Dialogue

Ray Bradbury has a ritual when it comes to hearing his characters' dialogue. As he wakes up, he lies in bed and listens to the voices in his head (which he calls his "morning theater"). Characters talk to one another and when their conversation reaches a certain pitch of excitement, he races out of bed to run and trap them before they are gone.

One truth writers eventually discover is that inspiration strikes at the most inopportune times, usually when you are in an important meeting, engaged in another activity, or don't have access to a pen.

The reason is that creativity is a result of a relaxed state, when we are not thinking about our story and preoccupied with another activity.

If your character does not start speaking when you are sitting down at the computer, ready to work, learn how to tease out his voice.

When you have a few spare minutes at work or are walking around the park, visualize your character and ask him how he's doing. Instead of writing down his response, as you would in your character diary, just open your ears. How does he talk? What does he say? Does his inflection reflect a social class or region you hadn't considered? Does it work? If so, can you rewrite his background so the backstory and accent fit?

What's interesting about storytelling is that often enough it's our characters who create themselves. When we, their creators, are off target they give us messages they need to be rewritten.

When you get your character speaking, continue to ask him open-ended questions about his feelings on politics, hot restaurants, and anything you can think of. Scribble notes to yourself about how he uses words. Does your character use "filler words" such as "like" or "you know what I'm saying?" Have you heard people speak like him before? Who were they? What is the similarity between them?

Developing the Art of listening

To write great dialogue, you'll have to become a professional eavesdropper. Get into the habit of hanging out at coffee places or restaurants alone. Listen to what's being said and how it's being said. If the conversation is between two people, try to figure out who has the power in the relationship. If you are eavesdropping on a dating couple, try to guess if they will stay together or they won't, and why.

In restaurants, you can gather an enormous amount of information about a person by the words and tone he uses when he addresses a waiter. Recently I overheard the frustration in a woman's voice when she only wanted to order an appetizer at an upscale restaurant where three courses were usually the norm. "I'm just going to have the salad," she fluttered nervously. "Is that all right?"

Now, ask yourself what this statement, said in a nervous, fluttery tone of voice, tells you about a character? Contrast it to the voice of a confident woman in a business suit and briskly announcing to the waiter: "I'd like a salad please! And I expect it with dressing on the side and extra tomato!" then dismissing him in a glance.

Once, while standing at a traffic light in Beverly Hills, I overheard the conversation of a man next to me advising a friend about his new carpet. "Don't buy the color white," he warned. "It shows the dirt." Now I didn't know anything about this person, but from his line of dialogue, I got the impression he was the type to sweep things under the rug, both literally and figuratively, and I would be hesitant to visit his home as a dinner guest. All that gleaned from just one line! Such is the power of dialogue.

How The Profession of Your Character Influences Dialogue

Have you noticed how people's professions or hobbies heavily influences the way they speak and the words they use? Educators tend to speak in a professorial way. People in the stock market use lingo more commonly used on the trading floor to pepper their speech in casual conversation.

When you write dialogue for your characters, be sure to take into consideration the language of their professions. Consider yourself, your spouse, and friends who work in professions other than your own. If you know any teachers, they're probably very good explainers and are concerned that you fully understand what they're telling you. A person in finance may talk a great deal about the "market," things "shooting up," "going for broke," etc. Asked how he's feeling after an injury, he might well say "on the rise" while a seamstress might say "on the mend."

Take a scene from the film *Saturday Night Fever* when Tony walks into the disco with his friends and older brother Frank, who is confused over family pressure to become a priest. Frank is thrilled to be in the disco after a lifetime of religion and restraint, and pleased that Tony is something of a celebrity in the club. When the dancers part to let Tony and the gang walk past, Frank blurts out this line of dialogue: "You're like Moses in the Red Sea… the crowd parts for you as you walk by."

As you can see, Frank's choice of words reflects his profession.

In the 1947 film *The Ghost and Mrs. Muir*, the character of Captain Gregg, played by Rex Harrison, is characterized by words that evoke the sea. His "tag" is the way he uses expressions such as "me ship" and "me house." Whenever possible, screenwriter Philip Dunne (adapter of the book by R. A. Dick) spiked the Captain's vocabulary with words a seaman would use, such as "whether you meet fair winds or foul" or "here's how you will chart your course."

Get into the habit of observing how many of the phrases friends and family use in casual conversation are influenced by their professions. A musician might express statements from his or her vantage point, such as "let's get onto a new riff" (to change the conversation) or "that vinyl ain't selling" (to tell a friend he's not buying what he has to say).

All About Patois
Our speech is a product of several factors: genetic programming (Julia Child's famously deep voice is a family trait), the region where we grew up; imitating the speech patterns of our parents; and adopting the slang of our friends or social group.

In England, it's possible to get a very specific sense of someone's socio-economic status and private schooling through their accents. In America, speech is also a popular indicator of social status – to a degree. In her taped conversations with Linda Tripp, Monica Lewinsky's voice emerged as one that could almost be characterized as a "Valley Girl" even though she was a 25-year-old, college-educated woman from Beverly Hills. As the original "Valley Girl" ("oh my God!") generation continues to age, their speech patterns remain ingrained. Typical "Valley Girl" expressions have gone national, in addition to new buzz words from the world of music and the media, and have come to be associated with the gay community, as well.

How to Give Each Character His or Her Own Voice

Do you ever make anonymous calls to stores, libraries, or other places of business you frequent and are surprised when the clerk on the other end of the phone recognizes you by your voice? Curious, isn't it.

Now, imagine the executive or reader who's settling down to read your script. If he is a freelance reader, he gets paid by the script so he wants to read it as quickly as possible. If he's an executive, you have to grab his attention on the first page, or else the script is history. One important way to guarantee his interest is to give each character his own unique voice that reflects his particular way of speaking, the expressions he uses, and how direct he is.

Creating Audio Tags and Markers

Think of the "aunt" character in the film, *Lost in Yonkers* (1993) as a perfect example of an audio tag. The aunt character had a very memorable way of speaking. She'd begin her sentence in a normal voice, but then run out of air so she'd have to "gasp" out the rest of it. Not only did it make her a distinctive character, but it injected the script with humor and appealed to an audience.

The aunt's "gasp" is what's called an audio tag. A tag marks your characters so specifically that you don't even need to read the character's name to be 100% sure who's speaking.

No need to give each and every one of your characters a gasp, wheeze, or the like, but you should give them one of the following:

- ✓ A word, slang, or expression they alone use.
- ✓ A way of arranging words in a sentence.
- ✓ A tone, urgent or passive, that characterizes virtually all their speech.
- ✓ A direct or indirect way of speaking.

Cameron Crowe's film *Jerry Maguire* tagged characters by bringing out key aspects of their personalities. The brash, ambitious character of Avery, Jerry's first girlfriend, always spoke in an excited frenzy, whether she was in the midst of sex or breaking up with him and punching him out for good measure. Laurel, the older, wiser sister of Jerry's secretary/love interest Dorothy Boyd, spoke from the shrill vantage point of a woman who's burnt out on men and either wants to save her sister grief, or is unconsciously envious that Dorothy has a man in her life.

The film *When Harry Met Sally* (1989) also featured audio tags and markers that emerged as reflections of the personalities of the central characters. Harry (played by actor Billy Crystal) had a wry, sardonic, know-it-all voice that underscored the fact he felt himself to be intellectually superior to everyone else. The contrast between Harry's often snide, unconsciously demeaning voice and Sally's defensive tone permeates every scene and positions their characters to perfection.

Spoken preferences also serve as markers, especially when they're repeated over and over throughout the script. In *Jerry Maguire*, African-American athlete Tidewell's expression "Show Me The Money" formed the idée fixe of the film.

The reason for using dialogue as an identification tag is so the audience can get a "grasp" of the character as quickly as possible.

It's best to avoid creating a tag on a whim, unless the character's voice and inflection suddenly "comes to you." Instead, tags should be born from the character's personality and history. If that voice you hear in your head corresponds to the character's past life, by all means, go for it!

For Fresher Dialogue

What is the secret of mesmerizing editors and script readers with your dialogue? When confronted, most editors just said they knew good dialogue when they saw it. Lucia Macro, executive editor at HarperCollins, believes that dialogue should flow naturally and sound "real" to the ear. She sometimes suggests to her authors that they read dialogue aloud so they can discover the natural cadence to their writing. Kate Duffy, senior editor at Kennsington Books, believes that great dialogue is credible and surprising.

Author Kathryn Lance feels that the key to making her characters sound different is to know them deeply and predict how they would speak in given situations. For her children's books, she likes to get into the mood for dialogue by watching sci-fi programs on the WB network. The snappily written ones help her pick out the rhythms of today's teens. Author Bill Neugent makes his characters sound different by making their voices mirror their characters, e.g., arrogant and high-brow, impatient, military, deliberative. He feels the successful route to fresher dialogue is to pretend that you're talking – show naked emotions, and be both provocative and entertaining.

The one element everyone agrees on is that dialogue in screenplays and novels is more than simply communicating information. Screen the film *All About Eve* and listen to the crisp dialogue, particularly of the Addison DeWitt character. You will quickly notice that it's not the words DeWitt uses, but the calculated way in which he uses them.

While you must always be true to the personalities of your characters, challenge them. Give their words bite and shades of meaning. Exceptional dialogue is your winning ticket to fame and fortune in the writing world.

◆ CHAPTER SUMMARY ◆

In this chapter you learned:

1. In the film industry, gatekeepers first scan scripts for dialogue.

2. You must take personality style into account as you shape dialogue for your characters.

3. Voices have personality.

4. That if backstory must be articulated through dialogue, keep it at a minimum and make every effort to work around it.

5. To give characters their own dialogue tag to make them unique.

◆ ASSIGNMENTS ◆

1. If you currently are working on a story, pay particular attention to how each character speaks according to character type.

2. See or rent a film and, after assigning a particular type to the characters, notice how well their dialogue matches their personality styles.

3. Listen to people in a café and, without looking at them, assign them personality styles based on dialogue alone.

4. Devote a section of your notebook to writing down ideas for your characters' dialogue tags based on overhearing expressions around you.

◆ CHAPTER SEVEN ◆

INSIDER SECRETS TO GET PAST THE GATEKEEPER

In the past six chapters, you've learned how to develop and even manifest characters using a variety of innovative methods. Your notebook should be brimming with bits of dialogue, dreams, and observations about your characters.

Once you work this material into a script or novel, it will likely be read by a reader, story analyst, junior editor, or intern (for convenience, we will refer to them as "gatekeepers") at a studio, production company, agency, or publishing house.

From your desk, it may be difficult to imagine how your material would be read. What are they looking for? What turns gatekeepers on – *and off*? Who are these people, anyway, and what can you do to inspire them to recommend your material to their bosses?

Step 1: Seducing the Gatekeeper
Gatekeepers come in a variety of age ranges and levels of experience. With the possible exception of staff studio analysts (who are unionized, well paid, and often make the job a career position) one can make the assumption that most gatekeepers are young. Therefore, they were born in the MTV generation and have short attention spans.

Another assumption we can make is that story analysis is a highly individual activity, and what appeals to one gatekeeper in terms of your writing style may not appeal to another. Beyond that, some gatekeepers may read your submission with rapt interest despite spelling errors and sloppy formatting, while another gatekeeper would consider it grounds for an immediate pass.

Bottom line? It's important to read through your material with the eye of a young, possibly impatient, time-pressed, overworked gatekeeper. Take notes as you go through your material, making sure the pace moves briskly, any exposition or description is clear, visual, and necessary, and most important, that the gatekeeper develops an emotional relationship with your key characters.

Professional speakers know that in order for an audience to internalize their messages they must make that all-important emotional connection.

If you have ever spoken in a public arena, you are keenly aware when your audience begins to lose interest with you and your material. Loss of interest can be as mild as people scrolling their Blackberries for messages or reading a magazine, to outright heckling or simply getting up and leaving the room. Yet when they first assembled in the room to hear you speak, they were willing to give you an hour of their time to hear what you had to say.

When you submit your script to a gatekeeper, it is a similar situation. Gatekeepers are perfectly willing to give your material an hour or more of their time, and hope to be dazzled and transported from their offices, reading typewritten words, to the vividly colorful world of your characters.

Therefore, your characters must engage and seduce the gatekeeper as expertly as the most dynamic motivational speakers, who create an emotional bonds using eye contact, movement, vivid, emotionally charged language, and face, vocal, and hand gestures to enhance the clarity of their messages.

So, what are the elements that would motivate gatekeepers to become obsessed with characters? As a starting point, here are some ideas.

1. Universal Characters

Bridget Jones (heroine of the book/film *Bridget Jones Diary*) touched the hearts of millions of women across the world who could relate to her dieting, self-confidence issues, and romantic hopes and dreams

A dozen years earlier, women related to Melanie Griffith's character in *Working Girl* because she represented the collective desire to jump off the track of a dead-end job, relationship, and life and hitch one's engine to a more fulfilling life, job, and romance. And via Julia Robert's character in *Pretty Woman*, females felt encouraged that, whatever their current circumstances, a Prince Charming is around the corner to sweep them off to fairyland.

A successful universal character must be just like us, but "us" in the most idyllic light. Author Kate Flora believes there are two sets of qualities which make characters universal.

"The first are those characters who are 'larger than life' who can do all the things we've dreamed of or longed to do. Readers long for heroes (and anti-heroes, such as Hannibal Lecter) who are compelling and fascinating. The other type of character who becomes universal is a character who is deeply ordinary, or 'like us' who faces life's difficulties and survives them a wiser, or changed, person."

2. Extreme Likeability

There was a time in the late 80s when virtually every script had a few opening pages in which two buddy characters engaged in witty repartee before the third page, when they were suddenly called off to rescue a speeding bus or otherwise save the world. The humor on these opening pages was self-deprecating, and subliminally served to showcase the dynamics of the buddy relationship, especially the character who is the "top gun."

Likeability does not need to be formulaic, but you should give careful thought to establishing why an audience would find your protagonist sympathetic and likeable. To that end, your character should connect with the gatekeeper in the first page, in "love at first sight fashion."

To make your character likeable, ask yourself why you have responded positively and immediately to a new acquaintance over the years. Usually, it's because that person has the traits we wish we could possess, or because (in the sense of a love interest) they have the qualities we personally admire and find highly attractive.

Chances are, the stranger you encountered didn't have to tell you the story of his life in order to get you to sympathize with him. Instead, he proved himself by a simple action you found admirable. Let your character charm the gatekeeper in a similar fashion with actions, not words.

Actions that render a character likeable can also be simple. Consider Sandra Bullock's character in the film *Speed*. All she basically did was exchange a pleasant hello with the bus driver in an opening scene, and the audience bonded with her instantly.

In director Alfred Hitchcock's *Rebecca* (1940, novel by Daphne Du Maurier) the future second wife of Maxim de Winter first endears herself to her audience as a young, inexperienced girl caught up in a wealthy, sophisticated world. Why do we empathize with her? Because most of us have been young and inexperienced and in unfamiliar situations and can relate to her situation. The contrast between the girl's innocent freshness and the jaded audacity of her employer also motivates an audience to be protective of her.

A terrified Rebecca and the housekeeper, Mrs. Danvers

3. A Heroic Nature

Kevin Costner immediately emerged as a heroic character in the opening scene of *Dances with Wolves* (1990) when we witness his interaction with the troops and witness his noble, peace making qualities even before the Indians enter the picture.

Heroism is not only confined to the battlefield. In the film *Jerry Maguire*, we very quickly witness protagonist Tom Cruise's heroic nature when he decides to leave the insincerity of corporate life behind and run his own shop, despite the significant opposition.

4. Eccentric, Quirky Characters Who Earn Our Empathy

As you have discovered, readers and viewers are drawn to attractive, likeable characters with whom we can empathize.

The fictional Bridget Jones, Holly GoLightly, and even Penny Lane from the film *Almost Famous* are just a few "outside the norm" characters we are compelled to root on, mostly because they march to the tune of their own drummers.

Step 2: Motivating Gatekeepers to Recommend Your Material

One of the most popular classes I teach is called "The first 10 pages" as many readers will only give your work 10 pages (or, often, two pages) to read "seriously," form an opinion on the material, and then skim to complete the coverage or reader's report (note: this is a form readers use to synopsize, score, and comment on your material).

So, the question is, how can you protect your work from being dismissed in the first few pages?

Ken Atchity and Chi-Li Wong, in their book *Writing Treatments that Sell*, offer a list of helpful first-act advice, designed to keep the reader heavily involved in your story.

1. Introduce the protagonist in a way that makes him immediately relatable to the audience, someone we care about and whom we root on;
2. Announce the protagonist's mission in the story in the form of an inciting incident or problem he must solve;
3. Set up the mood, the movie's tone, its setting and its stakes;
4. Suggest why this story is important to all of us – the central question, theme, metaphor, or conflict that will be explored throughout the movie;
5. Introduce the subplot or secondary action line that complements or conflicts with the protagonist's main action line;

6. Introduce the antagonist, the protagonist's chief obstacle;

7. Introduce a major event that turns the protagonist around completely (what he wants in life is challenged, and now he must react) and launches him into Act 2.

Screenwriting professor Lew Hunter advises screenwriters that the first page better sing. "The character has got to jump off the page, grab the reader by the throat, and nail him against the wall until the end of the screenplay."

Starting at the closest point to the main action or conflict is imperative, says Hunter. "The first page has to compel the reader – every character should have a structure of individuality. We must have a sense of conflict and what the character wants."

Before beginning to write, Hunter advises writers to have their characters clearly delineated in their minds. Who are they? What have they done? What are their dreams? What is the hero or heroine trying to get?

By way of example, Hunter refers to the film, *Butch Cassidy and the Sundance Kid*, stating that Butch and the Kid simply wanted things to be the way they used to be, which motivated their journey to Bolivia.

Hunter says the opening scene of *Butch Cassidy* sets the story up nicely, as it begins with a sense of who Butch is, and that the story will revolve around issues of law and order. On page 17, notes Hunter, the first act ends when it's suggested: "Let's go to Bolivia where we can do what we do best."

Finally, Hunter advises adding energy to the script. "You should write dialogue and description with judicious use of short, colorful, descriptive words that demonstrate that you have poetry in your soul." Brevity is essential, Hunter advises, quoting a line from *Escape from Alcatraz* (1979) in which Clint Eastwood's character was asked "How was your childhood?" and Eastwood's one-word answer – "short" – says everything the audience needs to know.

Screenwriter Allison Burnett says "when people read scripts they go into dream states so they feel they are in a movie. Your script must be visual and auditory, so they hear it and see it." Burnett discourages intruding on that experience with cute commentary (via descriptions) so the script reader is completely transported.

Also, advises Burnett, "make the reading experience as pleasant as possible. The form should be clean and perfect, with no distracting typos. Most important, everything must be clear – you don't want the reader to miss subtleties.

"For example, let's say that a guy and girl are sexually attracted to one another, but their conversation is about a baseball game. As a result, the dialogue might sound trite and the reader would be jarred from the experience and wonder "why is the author giving time to a meaningless conversation?"

Burnett suggests clarifying description in the form of "John and Mary walk down the street. Although they speak of other things, there is an underlying sexual chemistry."

To keep the reader in the desired dream state, Burnett advises against camera angles, overwriting, and description, and suggests that you really work the words you do use for description to render them as condensed and as clear as possible, as pleasing to hear as poetic prose. "Condense, condense, and condense," he advises.

Screenwriter David Tausik adds that the secret of mesmerizing story analysts is to present story information quickly, and in a clear, vibrant, succinct way. "For example, when you watch a film, a single visual image can say 1000 words. Even if the character is simply standing in front of the Empire State Building – or Main Street, USA – you automatically get a sense of the character and his world without his having to say a thing. Translating that visual image into a script requires many words and lines of description, which readers tend to skim. With wordiness you risk confusing the reader. The first thing a reader or executive thinks when opening a script is 'Who is the character?' and 'What is this story about?'"

Tausik suggests you answer these questions as clearly and cleanly as possible to orient the reader into the world of your story, and adds that the opening pages should be rewritten many times, perhaps tested on others for clarity.

Beverly Gray (author *Roger Corman: Blood-Sucking Vampires, Flesh-Eating Cockroaches, and Driller Killers*; *Ron Howard: From Mayberry to the Moon… and Beyond*; and more) UCLA screenwriting instructor, screenwriter, and former story editor for Concorde New Horizon Pictures adds: "A reader or development executive wants to be instantly drawn into the world of a story. It's important that this world be both convincing and interesting.

"From the first scene description onward, it must be clear that the writer knows what he or she is talking about. For example, a hospital or police station setting must be introduced in language that suggests the writer's knowledge of the inner workings of these locales, as well as the lingo that goes with them."

Richard Walter, chair of the Graduate Screenwriting program at UCLA, feels that it's crucial to offer "audience worthy" characters. He also warns against using parenthetical remarks under the character's name to describe the attitude or anything about the character. "A character is what he says and does. Characters exist in the screenplay without add-ons."

To get first hand information about what studio story analysts look for in a script, Keith Davis, story analyst/consultant at Columbia Pictures, was kind enough to agree to an interview.

Q: Keith, what qualities do you like to see in the first few pages of a script? Can you offer any hands-on advice to help writers ensure their opening pages sing?

A: Try to set the genre and tone of your script as soon as possible, letting the reader know what he's going to be reading, and allowing him to settle into the story you want to tell him.

Watch several different movie genres (and several examples of your script's genre) to see how other writers do this, but generally speaking, it's accomplished more through imagery and action than via dialogue. In fact, even if dialogue accompanies the action, try to keep it concise and resist the temptation to top load your story with exposition and information.

Think of yourself as the host of a party, setting a mood for your guests (your readers). If a guest has just arrived at the party and is trying to figure out the vibe of the room, and see who else is there, he's not ready to take in and remember too many details.

Q: Keith, what immediately engages your interest in a script?

A: I'm always impressed with any writer, in any medium, who tells his story with economy. Screenwriters, as you're working in a specific format, in a relatively set number of pages, try using mainly nouns and verbs and limiting the use of adjectives and adverbs.

If your idea, plot, characters, and conversation are compelling, you won't need to pump them up with qualifiers. (In fact, the overuse of adjectives and adverbs takes up space and slows your momentum.)

When you're setting a scene, don't try to do the work of the director, the art director, the set decorator, the costume designer, the makeup artist, etc. Unless you absolutely need a detailed description, or are trying for a unique/complex effect, establish the scene succinctly, then play it out. Similarly, try to limit your characters' dialogue, conveying their emotions instead through action and reaction.

Q: Is there a checklist you would give screenwriters before they submit their scripts?

A: It's impossible to have a perspective on, and be objective about, your own script — especially if you've just completed it. You're just too close to the material.

Before officially submitting the script to an agent, producer, or (especially) a studio, try to get some feedback on it from three people whose opinions you trust, then listen carefully to how they respond. You're don't have to agree with their opinions, or make changes based on what they say; ultimately, it's still your script and your vision.

Seeing your work through someone else's eyes is instructive, as you can test if they received the "message" you were trying to send. If you receive the same comments about certain elements, those elements are worth reexamining. Even if you disagree with the readers' ideas for changes, those ideas may lead you to make improvements of your own.

If you don't know people whose review and criticism of your script would be helpful, think about taking a screenwriting class and "workshopping" your script with the teacher and other students. In sum: don't submit your first draft; submit your rewrite... or maybe your rewrite polish.

Q: Can you say a few words about what warms you to a character early on? Can you speculate on the qualities a character needs to have in order to make an emotional connection with the reader?

A: When you're reading a script, the traits you like to see in characters are basically the same traits to which you respond in real-life people.

The problem, of course, is that when you're meeting people in real life, you react first to the way they look, and take cues from their facial expressions on how they're feeling and what they're thinking. Even if a script describes a character in some depth (and in truth, it probably shouldn't, as that treads on the job of the casting director), you don't get the same cues from reading about the person as you would from seeing him.

So, think about what appeals to — or amuses or annoys or repels or scares — you about the people you meet, aside from their looks. Their physical agility or lack of it... their dedication or indifference to their jobs... a specific sense of humor... the way they relate to, and treat, other people... their style of speaking and responding... their perspective on themselves and the world and people around them... their degree of honesty, ingenuity, courage, loyalty, and willingness to change or take chances.

Q: How do senior executives look at "weekend read" scripts as opposed to the way a story analyst would look at them?

A: In contrast to the late 1980s and early 1990s, my sense is that "Weekend Read" is no longer the place where most supposedly "hot" spec scripts are reviewed. At Columbia, spec scripts come in all week long (and often have to be read overnight, by both analysts and execs), and weekend reading seems to be mostly of new drafts of projects already in development. These methods make more sense: spec scripts can be showcased, rather than stockpiled; and projects can be reviewed more thoroughly by the creative group. When you read a spec script, the initial decision is whether or not to buy it. When you read a project, your comments are more specific, focused on improving the already-bought material, with the goal of turning it into a movie.

Giving Your Characters Depth

All sources interviewed stressed the importance of giving characters depth and originality. Many aspiring and working screenwriters and novelists will agree it's easier said than done.

However, I'll share a technique I use in "real life" that has helped me create characters that readers can empathize with.

The technique started when I realized the importance of being extremely friendly and positive with people who, on a gut, unconscious level, disturbed me with their negative energy.

Faking friendliness for the sake of appearances didn't work. So, employing the #1 rule of fiction that even the most evil villain has to have some positive, redeeming characteristics, I tried hard to think about some likeable traits of the individual(s) in question.

In the end, I had to roll back the years and use my vivid imagination to imagine a scene from this individual's childhood that portrayed him in a positive light. I imagined his mother was taking him for an ice cream on a warm summer day. His excitement at choosing among the flavors was palpable. I saw his nose pressed against the cold glass display case, and had to admit the scene was adorable and he came across as extremely cute.

After internalizing that imaginary scene, I found myself smiling at him in a genuine way, because I didn't see "him" and his negativity, I saw the small adorable child he was once (at least, in my imagination).

I discovered also that if this type of visualization works in real life, it can work to add depth and dimension to fictional characters, as well.

So, the next time you are stuck, try to think about an incident in the character's past. Once you can vividly see it, you can Mind Map or brainstorm corresponding traits in your character.

Special Note on Comedy

Screenwriter John Blumenthal (the films *Blue Streak* [1999], *Short Time* [1990] and the novel *What's Wrong with Dorfman*) suggests that comedic screenplays require heightened attention to story set-up and characterization.

"You must engage the reader by being as funny as possible in the first few pages, especially where dialogue is involved. Dialogue can often illustrate character more effectively than description. Remember, your job is to entertain – both in the sense of entertaining whoever is reading the script, as well as creating an entertaining story for film."

Blumenthal also advises to keep the pace brisk and the structure tight, so that the reader has a sense of the story as soon as possible.

Coverage and the Readers Report

Story analysts in studios use a specific form in which to record their reactions to your screenplay. It is called "coverage" or a reader's report and typically consists of four pages. The first page is a computer-generated form with spaces for the author, title, log line (for example, the sentence the TV Guide uses to describe the theme of the movie), and brief comments (usually two sentences).

On this initial page, there is also a grid where readers can rank elements such as characterization, dialogue, structure, etc., on a 1-5 scale. Finally, on this front page the reader will either recommend that the project receive a review from a more senior executive, or be passed and rejected.

After the front page is a two-page, single-spaced synopsis of your story. Finally, the last page of the coverage includes a full page of comments.

Below is a sample of studio coverage so you can see how your work could be evaluated. While it is important to make your script as easy to understand and enjoyable to read as possible, never be discouraged if your script is rejected. It could mean the reader was distracted, inexperienced, or the timing just wasn't right. Many projects, passed on for years by major studios, have gone on to make hundreds of millions of dollars, including *The Talented Mr. Ripley* (1999) and even John Grisham's *The Firm* (1993).

Typical Studio Coverage Cover Sheet

Title:	Form:
Author:	Pages:
Time:	Publisher:
Location:	Submitted by:
Genre:	Submitted to:
Elements:	Analyst:
Date:	

Logline: (7- 15-word single-spaced sentence describing the basic concept of the material, such as you might see in TV Guide).

Short Summary: (A short, single-spaced summary of the material, no longer than four sentences, based on your one-page summary after your synopsis).

(Rating Grid – readers will check a box for each element)

	Excellent	Good	Fair	Poor
Characterization				
Dialogue				
Structure				
Storyline				
Production Values				

Budget: __low __medium __high

Recommend ___
Pass   ___

What Analysts Consider
Character is key.

Second, readers consider the concept. 1994's *The Terminator* (a cyborg arrives from the future to kill someone in the present) is a good example of a strong concept and hook.

Dialogue is important, as is structure, but as you've already discovered in the course of this book, the reader has pretty much decided if he's sufficiently involved in the story by page 10.

If the reader isn't grabbed by page 10, the script is "covered" but mentally the reader is deciding how he is going to legitimize the pass (i.e., structure is weak, dialogue is bland).

The first thing the reader writes is the two-page synopsis, which basically tells the story as if you were telling it to a small child, from beginning to end.

Next, he tackles the comments page, which usually follows the formula of a first paragraph that summarizes the good and bad points of the story. The second paragraph usually focuses on characterization, the third paragraph dialogue, and the fourth paragraph structure and other elements. The fifth paragraph, once again, summarizes the reason for the pass or recommend.

The very best readers know that the attention spans of executives are short, and try to make the synopses fun and informative to read.

By this, I mean that they compare the story to other films, discuss characters in terms of types, and keep the language simple, colorful, and easy to follow. Many executives reportedly read directly from the comments page when they phone an agent to explain why they are passing on the script, so savvy readers train themselves to write so that their comments can be given verbatim.

Note that when Hollywood readers analyze manuscripts or books with regard for film adaptation, the same basic elements (save for structure) apply, with characterization and concept key points.

Step 3: Impressing Senior Executives
(NY Publishing Houses & Hollywood)
When your script or book is recommended in coverage, many possibilities can occur. In the publishing world, often a senior editor herself reads the manuscript and if she passionately falls in love with it, presents the book in a meeting of editors and sales/marketing staff. If the sales/marketing people don't think it can sell, the project can be dropped unless the editor has incredible power or seniority.

I asked a number of editors in New York publishing houses what they look for in manuscripts, so you can write to their specifications. Anna Genoese, assistant editor at Tom Doherty Associates, LLC, where she acquires for both the Tor and Forge Books, suggests that authors sketch the characters out with particular details "so that readers can connect the dots and get the whole picture rather than giving readers every single detail of the characters' life histories."

This is sound advice. In the film industry, you risk losing immediate credibility with readers when you flood the opening pages with your character's life history. Again, your goal is to inspire curiosity and motivate your audience to keep turning the pages to find out more about your characters.

Another key point to keep in mind, for both films and books, is to reveal characterization via action. For example, if an important story point concerns the fact your character disrespects others and has a phobia about other people's germs, you would not want to describe this in exposition, or possibly even in dialogue.

In the film *As Good as it Gets* (1997), Jack Nicholson plays a character of this description, but his peculiar habits are conveyed via the way he insists on plastic utensils when eating at restaurants, and speaks rudely to others without consideration of their feelings.

Jack Nicholson's Melvin takes out plastic, germ-free utensils

"When discussing the mechanics of writing with authors," says Lucia Macro, "my constant frustration — and I suspect theirs — is that I don't necessarily believe that you can teach or explain what makes characters jump off a page — I can just point out to them when a character is acting inconsistently or when they aren't drawing me to them.

Of course, as an editor what I want are characters whom I can believe in, whom I can relate to, and whom I can start to think of as 'real.' They need to have the same human foibles and quirks as the rest of us — they need to share in the same hopes and dreams."

Kensington Senior Editor Kate Duffy suggests the hallmark of good characterization "would be the author's ability to capture and convey her thorough understanding of, and empathy for, her characters whether in descriptive prose, dialogue, or action."

In the film world, producers, studio executives, and directors are looking for all of the above, plus two other key elements. First and most important is a character (and story) who fits the demographics of the movie-going audience.

Remember, as well, that film character leads have to be "good guys" and it's imperative that the audience root them on in their endeavors. When an audience sees its favorite movie hero on the screen 10-feet high, psychologically it connects with that heroic character, and vicariously experiences the agony and ecstasy of being that character, and achieving the victory that the character worked for and won at the end of the story.

During the movie mogul era, studio chiefs like Sam Goldwyn hired their lead actors and actresses based on surveys that suggested which actress/actor the audience would most want to be romantic with. To a large extent, sex appeal is still important today, whether the character is simply dazzling to look at, or is written so well he enjoys seductive powers over other characters. Consider that "charm" is another word for seduction, and your responsibility as a writer is to make your character so mesmerizing he will entrance an audience.

The second element is that the protagonist could be perceived as a good vehicle for a top star, such as Cameron Diaz or Johnny Depp. Managers and agents are in the business of pleasing their star clients and toward that end must feed them a steady diet of appropriate scripts. Write your script with that actor in mind, and then submit your script to the agency representing the actor with a cover letter that explains the story and your qualifications.

By the same token, keep your eyes open for young, energetic up-and-comers mentioned in the trades, especially actors who are getting a lot of attention in independent films. Consider writing roles that would represent the "next step" for them in challenging parts that suit their types and personalities.

Understanding the Studio Packaging System

Agencies like to sell studios "packages" with their stars attached. The reason is that they can make triple – or more – commissions by placing the stars, director, and screenwriter in one package.

Major talent agencies such as International Creative Management (ICM) and William Morris have departmental meetings at least once a month to discuss "available properties" and stars/directors in need of work. A logline, synopsis, and short description of top roles in the screenplay are briefly presented by individual agents, so that agents representing talent (i.e., actors, actresses, directors) can take note of good matches for their personal clients.

Trends Are Key

In the film world especially, screenplays that reflect current or upcoming cultural trends have an extra advantage. On a superficial level, the word "trends" is used to mean the hot genre of the moment. During various periods studios bought buddy stories, body-exchange stories, coming-of-age stories, etc.

But on a deeper level, the word "trend" is meant to reflect how well the writer has captured the *zeitgeist* of the moment through his characters and his story.

Webster's dictionary defines the word "zeitgeist" as *"The spirit of the time; the general intellectual and moral state or temper characteristic of any period of time."*

For example, the Renaissance had a certain spirit as illustrated in its art, its technology, mathematics, and religious outlook everywhere. All these phenomena which characterize the 16th century could be summed up as the spirit of the Renaissance – the sum of ideas common to many people. One could also speak of the spirit of Marxism or Socialism when it would be the common, collective idea for the whole group.

The film *Dances with Wolves* touched a cord with its target audience, as well as with the gatekeepers who saw how well the story and characters reflected the collective zeitgeist of the year 1990, when it was released at the height of that era's economic downturn.

Savvy gatekeepers took one look at the property in 1988 and could see that film-going Americans, disillusioned after the high-flying, over-the-top 80s, would respond favorably to a period story in which a young Army Lieutenant takes a spiritual journey and rediscovers his own core values.

So far, so good. But how do you spot trends, especially if you're writing a story that will be marketed months or years from today?

One secret is to make a key point of carefully listening to what is going on in the world around you. This is how futurist Faith Popcorn forecasts trends, by looking at the collective zeitgeist of our society, putting seemingly disconnected elements together, and forecasting what's next.

Study new television commercials or analyze the winners of the Clio advertising awards, as the talent, wit, and trend-tracking research of advertising departments can give you a good indication of what will interest Americans in the coming months and years. Look to the worlds of music, fashion, and literature – what are their commonalities?

Or, you could keep your eye on the various "in and out" lists in *Vanity Fair* and other magazines. Whatever is "in" today will morph into a new trend that is either its polar opposite, or pushes the envelope by taking the trend to the next level. Try to keep current with people in various age groups, especially teens and the college set. What are they wearing and doing?

Your scripts and persona must reflect your talent, and telegraph the fact that you are an individual up to date on the latest trends – especially when it comes to taking pitch meetings with producers.

How can you sharpen your skills?

Make it a habit to scan a wide variety of magazine headlines at the news stand.

Mentally try to write a cohesive paragraph that effectively puts its finger on the pulse of America today using headlines from a wide variety of dissimilar, popular magazines, such as *Vogue, Time, Newsweek, Mens' Health*, and *Cosmo*.

When you do, you will see you are in a better vantage point for seeing the zeitgeist of American society today and predicting trends tomorrow.

◆ CHAPTER SUMMARY ◆

In this chapter you learned:

1. What motivates a gatekeeper to say "yes!"

2. Elements of a universal character.

3. Ways of keeping the "gatekeeper" immersed in your story.

4. Elements of a reader's report (story coverage).

5. Why understanding – and predicting – trends are essential.

◆ ASSIGNMENTS ◆

1. This week, decide on the specific target market your story is to reach. If your target market is teenage girls, for example, train yourself to notice trends. What are they wearing? What movies are they seeing? Whom do the teen magazines say are their heartthrobs?

2. See more films in the theaters or on DVD. Mentally, or with a notebook, analyze how the scenes open and why you become involved with the characters. Novelists, do the same thing with books.

3. Take your main character out of the computer and into the world. Observe (in your imagination) the reaction that other people make about your character.

4. Screenwriters, look at the first 10 pages of several screenplays (many film schools have script libraries). Analyze what draws your interest in both the plot and character. Make notes.

Epilogue

Are your characters beginning to whisper their secrets? Are they paying you visits from their magical spheres?

I enjoyed sharing ways to help you establish a closer relationship with your characters via dreams, dialogue, diaries, treasure maps, and the myriad other unconventional ways we can give "imaginary" characters life and physicality.

You will find the More-Personality system a powerful tool in your writing arsenal. In the "real world" it is successfully used to help people understand the strengths and weaknesses of their own personality types so that they can improve communication with others and avoid conflicts. Conversely, in screenplays and novels, your objective is to *increase conflict*, so you will want to take the traits of your characters to the extreme and watch the fireworks.

In my seminars, I often open by asking attendees if concept, or characterization, is the most important element in a film. Though the response is almost always concept, I'm sure you now agree that character is the most important element in any story. One of the most enjoyable aspects of seeing films is to jump inside the body of another and experience life from a fresh new perspective. This is why it is so important to use all the techniques in this book to draw out the colorful nuances of your characters and make it fun and edifying to spend time with them.

I encourage you to sign up for my complimentary e-zine at *www.HollywoodScreenwriter.com*, and to e-mail me at *mdvari@HollywoodScreenwriter.com* with any comments or questions.

Onward and upward!

Marisa D'Vari

APPENDIX 1

List of films and TV shows discussed in this book, arranged in order of appearance:

Pretty Woman
Gone With the Wind
Jerry Maguire
All About Eve
Rocky
Cape Fear
Columbo (TV Series Starring Peter Falk)
A Beautiful Mind
The Birdcage
Chinatown
Wall Street
Dangerous Liasions
Silence of the Lambs
The Odd Couple (the classic film)
Blood and Sand
Reservoir Dogs
Butch Cassidy and the Sundance Kid
The Fisher King
The Ghost and Mrs. Muir
Queen of the Damned
Casablanca
Sea of Love
Flashdance
You've Got Mail
Basic Instinct
Fatal Attraction
Rear Window
Gosford Park
Working Girl
Rebecca (the film version directed by Hitchcock)
Dances with Wolves
As Good as it Gets

APPENDIX 2

Personality Quiz with Julia Roberts

Example: Letting "Vivian" from *Pretty Woman* Take the Quiz

For the purpose of example, let's let the character of Vivian, played by Julia Roberts in the film Pretty Woman, take the quiz.

For Question 1, she would answer A (Obstinate) over B (Beguiling) so we would assign the rank of "7" for A, "5" for B, "3" for C (Genial) and "1" for D (Docile).

A note on how Vivian would fill out Question 1. You might have initially thought she was more beguiling than obstinate, since she is attractive and charming. But underneath her pretty exterior lies a determined woman who drove the third act action by refusing to be second best, and holding out until she got an offer of marriage.

For Question 2, the letter B (Fun-loving) describes Vivian's character the most, so she would put the number "7" next to B. As Vivian is more aggressive (A) than agreeable or compliant, we would put a "5" next to A. Even though Vivian's really neither Agreeable (C) nor Compliant (D) we MUST assign a numerical quality to each, so let's make her Agreeable "3" over Compliant "1," again writing these numbers next to the letters that describe her best.

For Question 3, let us give Vivian a "7" for letter A, Courageous and a "5" for letter B, Ability to Dazzle. Let's give her "3" for C, Balanced, and "1" for Exact (D).

For Question 4, let's give her "7" for letter C (Amiable), "5" for A (Resolute), "3" for D (Guarded) and "1" for B (Scheming).

For the last Question 5, let's give Vivian "7" for B (Cheerful), "5" for C (Easy-Going), "3" for D (Scrupulous) and "1" for A (Demanding).

Now, we would total her score for A, which is 25. We would then put the number "25" in the quadrant marked "A" (top right).

Vivian's score for B is 27, so we will put the number "27" in the quadrant marked B in the lower right.

Vivian's score for C is 21, so we would put the number "21" in the quadrant marked C in the lower left.

Vivian's score for D is 7, so we would put this number in the upper left quadrant.

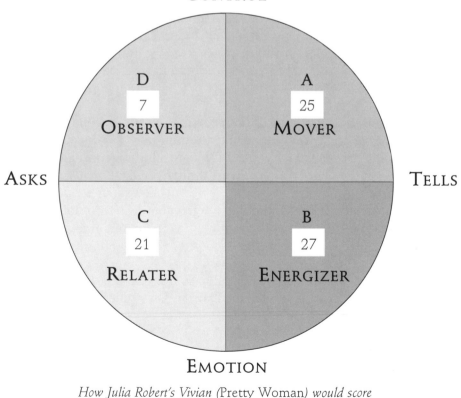

How Julia Robert's Vivian (Pretty Woman) would score

RESOURCES

Writers are so lucky to be living in today's computer age, when information can be received within an instant over the Internet. In this section you will find recommended books, trade publications, and other resources for jump starting your writing career.

Trade Publications

As discussed, it's important to learn as much as possible about your industry. *Screenwriters should subscribe to Variety* and *The Hollywood Reporter* or regularly read it in the library. Novelists should read *Publisher's Weekly* via subscription or at the library.

You can also get news from the Web sites, though it is limited.

The Hollywood Reporter, Daily and Weekly (323) 525-2000
(*www.hollywoodreporter.com*)

Publisher's Weekly   (646) 746-6758
(*www.PublishersWeekly.com*)

Variety, Daily and Weekly   (323) 857-6600
(*www.variety.com*)

Publications for Writers

Scr(i)pt   (410) 592-3466

Creative Screenwriter   (800) 727-6978
                                        or (323) 957-1405

Written By: (production of WGA)   (888) 974-8629

Writer's Digest (*www.WritersDigest.com*)

The Writer (*www.WriterMag.com*)

Romance Writers of America (*www.RWANational.org*)

These publications feature interviews with novelists, agents, feature and TV writers and are great sources for keeping in touch with the literary and filmmaking communities.

Consumer Publications

In addition, you might check out these consumer-oriented publications. The information is geared to the mass market, but you'll be able to put your finger on the pulse of the marketplace. You'll also get a sense of the market, what fans want to see, and how studios promote their films. Buy them on the stands or subscribe.

Premiere
Entertainment Weekly

Bookstores For Writers

While the major bookstores carry all or most of the books I recommend, bookstores that cater to the screenwriting trade offer more unusual or self-published books others don't. Besides, they're fun places to hang out, meet other writers, and the staff is well versed on the best books to buy.

Los Angeles

Samuel French Bookstore	(323) 876-0570
Book Soup	(310) 659-3410
Vromans	(626) 449-5320
Writer's Store	(866) 229-7483

New York

Drama Books	(212) 944 0595

San Francisco

City Lights	(415) 362-8193

Online Script Sales

If you live outside of L.A. and New York, here is where you can buy copies of scripts online.
www.hollywoodbookcity.com

Reading scripts is a great way to learn the rhythm and specific format for motion picture and television scripts. Start with scripts that have won Academy Awards for original screenplay for reference, and then read scripts similar to the genre you're writing that have done well in the box office.

If you plan to write for television, it's crucial to order at least one script for the show you want to write for, in order to study the format.

Internet Discussion Groups

Consider becoming a regular or a "lurker" on one of the many "listserv" discussion groups online, where you can interact with other screenwriters and novelists. You'll find answers to many of your questions, and possibly, someone to read your script or book before you send it out.

The easiest way to find them is to simply go to your favorite Internet search engine and type in something like "Internet Discussion Group + novelists" or "Internet Discussion Group + screenwriters" and click on the various listings.

Web Sites of Interest

The Internet has tens of thousands of great sites where you can find helpful information on writing. Below is a select sampling of only a few of my favorites.

www.imdb.com
This site is an incredible asset for instantly referencing films.

www.wga.org
The Writers Guild of America has limitless resources, articles, and is the center for a variety of great writing links.

www.SmokingGun.com
Great gossip about the world of film and publishing.

www.HollywoodScreenwriter.com
This is my own site, well stocked with articles, tips, and a sign-up box for our complimentary ezine.

www.mwp.com
This is the site for the publisher of this book, Michael Wiese Productions, which has great articles and a wealth of helpful books to round out your education.

Organizations
Women in Film	*www.wif.org*
Hollywood Scriptwriter's Network	*www.scriptwritersnetwork.org*
Sisters in Crime (for mystery writers)	*www.SinC.com*
Mystery Writers of America (for mystery writers)	*www.mysterywriters.org*
Romance Writers of America (for romance writers)	*www.rwanational.org*

Film-Oriented Libraries
Los Angeles is a city with several libraries devoted to film. Many library Web sites also have helpful articles and listing of events.

Writer's Guild of America	(323) 951-4000
www.wga.org	
American Film Institute (AFI)	(323) 856-7600
www.afionline.org	
Margaret Herrick Library	(310) 247-3035

Academy of Motion Picture Arts and Sciences
http://www.oscars.org/mhl/
USC Cinema-Television Library   (213) 740-8906
http://artscenter.usc.edu/cinematv/

Screenwriting & Writing Classes

Virtually every city in America offers screenwriting and/or novel writing classes at local universities. Increasingly, you also can take classes online from universities, bookstores, and Web sites.

With the thousands of listings, your best bet is to use an Internet search engine and plug in key words like "screenwriting classes + online) or (novel writing classes + online) and choose the class that meets your needs.

Screenwriting & Novel Writing Conferences

Conferences are great, because they give you the opportunity to absorb material and meet the kind of high-powered players you'll be connecting with later in your career.

A local conference will also give you the opportunity to network with other screenwriters and form a group where you can read one another's material, and share resources such as scripts and magazines.

One of the best conferences for screenwriters is *Words Into Pictures* offered by the Writer's Guild of America. You can find more information from the *www.wga.org* Web site.

Novelists are best advised to go to a writing conference dedicated to their niche. For example, mystery writers should go to the many mystery conferences that take place throughout the year. A good place to find out about them is to use the Internet search engines or visit Web sites sponsored by Mystery Writers of America (*http://www.mysterywriters.org/*) or Sisters in Crime (*http://www.SinC.com*). Romance writers can find conferences using search engines or learn details about the conference sponsored by the Romance Writers of America (*http://www.mystery-writers.org/*).

Recommended Books

Creativity & Publishing
◆ Atchity, Kenneth, *A Writer's Time*, Norton 1995
◆ Atchity, Kenneth; McKeown, Andrea; Mooney, Julie; *How to Publish Your Novel: A Complete Guide to Making the Right Publisher Say Yes,* 2004
◆ Poynter, Dan, *The Self-Publishing Manual: How to Write, Print, and Sell Your Own Book*, 14th Edition
◆ Ross, Tom and Marilyn, *Jump Start Your Book Sales: A Money-Making Guide for Authors, Independent Publishers and Small Press*, 1999.
◆ Ross, Marilyn, *Shameless Marketing for Brazen Hussies: 307 Awesome Money-Making Strategies for Savvy Entrepreneurs*
◆ Ross, Tom and Marilyn, *Complete Guide to Self Publishing: Everything You Need to Know to Write, Publish, Promote, and Sell Your Own Book,* (Self-Publishing 4th Edition)

Intuition, Dreams, Magic, and Spirituality
◆ Bonewits, Issac, *Real Magic*, Samuel Weiser Inc., 1989.
◆ Guiley, Rosemary Ellen, *The Dreamer's Way: Using Proactive Dreaming for Creativity and Healing*, Berkley Books, April 2004.
◆ Guiley, Rosemary Ellen, *Dreamspeak: How to Understand the Messages in Your Dreams*, 2001.
◆ Guiley, Rosemary Ellen, *Breakthrough Intuition: How to Achieve the Life of Abundance by Listening to the Voice Within*, 2001.
◆ Guiley, Rosemary Ellen, *The Encyclopedia of Dreams: Symbols and Interpretations*, 1995.
◆ Stevens, Jose (Ph.D.) and Lena, *Secrets of Shamanism: Tapping The Spirit Power Within You*, Avon, 1988.

Psychology

- Aziz, Robert, C.G., *Jung's Psychology of Religion and Synchronicity*, State University of New York Press, 1990.
- Jung, C.G., *Synchronicity*, First Princeton/Bolligen Paperback Edition, 1973.
- Stein, Murray, *Jung's Map of the Soul*, Open Court (a division of Carus Publishing Company) 1988.
- Von Franz, Marie-Louise, *On Divination and Synchronicity: The Psychology of Meaningful Chance*, Inner City Books, 1980.

Screenwriting

- Atchity, Ken and Chi-Li Wong, *Writing Treatments That Sell*, Henry Holt & Company, 2003.
- Cooper, Dona, *Writing Great Screenplays for Film and TV*, Arco (Second Edition), 1997.
- D'Vari, Marisa, *Script Magic: Subconscious Techniques to Conquer Writer's Block*, 2000.
- Field, Syd, *The Screenwriter's Problem Solver: How to Recognize, Identify, and Define Screenwriting Problems*, Dell Paperback, 1998
- Field, Syd, *The Screenwriter's Workbook*, Dell, 1984.
- Hague, Michael, *Writing Screenplays that Sell*, Harperperennial 1991
- Hunter, Lew, *Lew Hunter's Screenwriting 434*, Perigee, 1995
- McKee, Robert, *Story*, Harper Collins, 1997.
- Palumbo, Dennis, *Writing from the Inside Out*, Wiley, 2000.
- Vogler, Christopher, *The Writer's Journey*, Michael Wiese Productions. 1998
- Voytilla, Stuart, *Myth and the Movies: Discovering the Mythic Structure of Over 50 Unforgettable Films*, Michael Wiese Productions, 1999.

About the Author

Marisa D'Vari is a former entertainment industry executive (TriStar, MGM) who started her career in the motion picture literary department of International Creative Management.

President of Deg.Com Communications in Manhattan, D'Vari is a consultant to both writers and executives, as she uses techniques developed while working with writers (including the More-Personality™ system described in this book) to empower entrepreneurs, executives, and corporations through enhanced communication skills.

A national speaker and author of five books, D'Vari conducts keynote speeches and workshops for a wide variety of literary and screenwriting associations and conferences, in addition to the Institute of Management Consultants, the American Society of Association Executives, National Speakers Association, Boston Security Analysts Society, and Harvard University.

D'Vari's previous book for Michael Wiese Productions, *Script Magic: Subconscious Techniques to Conquer Writer's Block* (2000) has been translated into Korean and Japanese and her newest book for Career Press, *Building Buzz: How to Reach and Impress Your Target Audience,* is quickly becoming a best-seller.

To inquire about D'Vari's services, please contact her at *mdvari@deg.com* or read informative free articles on her Web site, *www.HollywoodScreenwriter.com.*

THE WRITER'S JOURNEY
2ND EDITION
MYTHIC STRUCTURE FOR WRITERS

CHRISTOPHER VOGLER

BEST SELLER
OVER 116,500 UNITS SOLD!

See why this book has become an international bestseller and a true classic. *The Writer's Journey* explores the powerful relationship between mythology and storytelling in a clear, concise style that's made it required reading for movie executives, screenwriters, playwrights, scholars, and fans of pop culture all over the world.

Both fiction and nonfiction writers will discover a set of useful myth-inspired storytelling paradigms (i.e., "The Hero's Journey") and step-by-step guidelines to plot and character development. Based on the work of Joseph Campbell, *The Writer's Journey* is a must for all writers interested in further developing their craft.

The updated and revised second edition provides new insights and observations from Vogler's ongoing work on mythology's influence on stories, movies, and man himself.

"This book is like having the smartest person in the story meeting come home with you and whisper what to do in your ear as you write a screenplay. Insight for insight, step for step, Chris Vogler takes us through the process of connecting theme to story and making a script come alive."
> — Lynda Obst, Producer
> Sleepless in Seattle, How to Lose a Guy in 10 Days
> Author, Hello, He Lied

"This is a book about the stories we write, and perhaps more importantly, the stories we live. It is the most influential work I have yet encountered on the art, nature, and the very purpose of storytelling."
> — Bruce Joel Rubin, Screenwriter
> Stuart Little 2, Deep Impact, Ghost, Jacob's Ladder

CHRISTOPHER VOGLER, a top Hollywood story consultant and development executive, has worked on such high-grossing feature films as *The Lion King*, *The Thin Red Line*, *Fight Club*, and *Beauty and the Beast*. He conducts writing workshops around the globe.

$24.95 | 325 PAGES | ORDER # 98RLS | ISBN: 0-941188-70-1

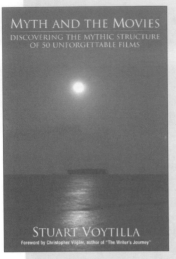

MYTH AND THE MOVIES
DISCOVERING THE MYTHIC STRUCTURE OF 50 UNFORGETTABLE FILMS

STUART VOYTILLA
FOREWORD BY CHRISTOPHER VOGLER
AUTHOR OF *THE WRITER'S JOURNEY*

BEST SELLER
OVER 15,000 UNITS SOLD!

An illuminating companion piece to *The Writer's Journey*, *Myth and the Movies* applies the mythic structure Vogler developed to 50 well-loved U.S. and foreign films. This comprehensive book offers a greater understanding of why some films continue to touch and connect with audiences generation after generation.

Movies discussed include *The Godfather, Some Like It Hot, Citizen Kane, Halloween, Jaws, Annie Hall, Chinatown, The Fugitive, Sleepless in Seattle, The Graduate, Dances with Wolves, Beauty and the Beast, Platoon,* and *Die Hard.*

"Stuart Voytilla's Myth and the Movies *is a remarkable achievement: an ambitious, thought-provoking, and cogent analysis of the mythic underpinnings of fifty great movies. It should prove a valuable resource for film teachers, students, critics, and especially screenwriters themselves, whose challenge, as Voytilla so clearly understands, is to constantly reinvent a mythology for our times."*
— *Ted Tally, Academy Award Screenwriter,* Silence of the Lambs

*"*Myth and the Movies *is a must for every writer who wants to tell better stories. Voytilla guides his readers to a richer and deeper understanding not only of mythic structure, but also of the movies we love."*
— *Christopher Wehner, Web editor*
The Screenwriters Utopia *and* Creative Screenwriting

*"*I've script consulted for ten years and I've studied every genre thoroughly. I thought I knew all their nuances – until I read Voytilla's book. This ones goes on my Recommended Reading List. A fascinating analysis of the Hero's Myth for all genres."
— *Lou Grantt,* Hollywood Scriptwriter Magazine

STUART VOYTILLA is a screenwriter, literary consultant, teacher, and author of *Writing the Comedy Film.*

$26.95 | **300 PAGES** | **ORDER # 39RLS** | **ISBN: 0-941188-66-3**

FILM & VIDEO BOOKS

Alone In a Room: Secrets of Successful Screenwriters
John Scott Lewinski / $19.95

Cinematic Storytelling: The 100 Most Powerful Film Conventions Every Filmmaker Must Know / Jennifer Van Sijll / $22.95

The Complete Independent Movie Marketing Handbook: Promote, Distribute & Sell Your Film or Video / Mark Steven Bosko / $39.95

Costume Design 101: The Art and Business of Costume Design for Film and Television / Richard La Motte / $19.95

Could It Be a Movie? How to Get Your Ideas Out of Your Head and Up on the Screen / Christina Hamlett / $26.95

Crashing Hollywood: How to Keep Your Integrity Up, Your Clothes On & Still Make It in Hollywood / Fran Harris / $24.95

Creating Characters: Let Them Whisper Their Secrets
Marisa D'Vari / $26.95

The Crime Writer's Reference Guide: 1001 Tips for Writing the Perfect Murder
Martin Roth / $17.95

Cut by Cut: Editing Your Film or Video
Gael Chandler / $35.95

Cut to the Chase: Forty-Five Years of Editing America's Favorite Movies
Sam O'Steen as told to Bobbie O'Steen / $24.95

Digital Cinema: The Hollywood Insider's Guide to the Evolution of Storytelling
Thom Taylor and Melinda Hsu / $27.95

Digital Editing with Final Cut Pro 4 (includes 45 minutes of DVD tutorials and sample footage) / Bruce Mamer and Jason Wallace / $31.95

Digital Filmmaking 101: An Essential Guide to Producing Low-Budget Movies
Dale Newton and John Gaspard / $24.95

Digital Moviemaking, 2nd Edition: All the Skills, Techniques, and Moxie You'll Need to Turn Your Passion into a Career / Scott Billups / $26.95

Directing Actors: Creating Memorable Performances for Film and Television
Judith Weston / $26.95

Directing Feature Films: The Creative Collaboration Between Directors, Writers, and Actors / Mark Travis / $26.95

Dream Gear: Cool & Innovative Tools for Film, Video & TV Professionals
Catherine Lorenze / $29.95

The Encyclopedia of Underground Movies: Films from the Fringes of Cinema
Phil Hall / $26.95

The Eye is Quicker Film Editing: Making a Good Film Better
Richard D. Pepperman / $27.95

Film & Video Budgets, 3rd Updated Edition
Deke Simon and Michael Wiese / $26.95

Film Directing: Cinematic Motion, 2nd Edition
Steven D. Katz / $27.95

Film Directing: Shot by Shot, Visualizing from Concept to Screen
Steven D. Katz / $27.95

The Film Director's Intuition: Script Analysis and Rehearsal Techniques
Judith Weston / $26.95

Film Production Management 101: The Ultimate Guide for Film and Television Production Management and Coordination / Deborah S. Patz / $39.95

Filmmaking for Teens: Pulling Off Your Shorts
Troy Lanier and Clay Nichols / $18.95

First Time Director: How to Make Your Breakthrough Movie
Gil Bettman / $27.95

From Word to Image: Storyboarding and the Filmmaking Process
Marcie Begleiter / $26.95

The Hollywood Standard: The Complete & Authoritative Guide to Script Format and Style / Christopher Riley / $18.95

The Independent Film and Videomakers Guide, 2nd Edition: Expanded and Updated / Michael Wiese / $29.95

Inner Drives: How to Write & Create Characters Using the Eight Classic Centers of Motivation / Pamela Jaye Smith / $26.95

Joe Leydon's Guide to Essential Movies You Must See: If You Read, Write About – or Make Movies / Joe Leydon / $24.95

Myth and the Movies: Discovering the Mythic Structure of 50 Unforgettable Films / Stuart Voytilla / $26.95

On the Edge of a Dream: Magic & Madness in Bali
Michael Wiese / $16.95

The Perfect Pitch: How to Sell Yourself and Your Movie Idea to Hollywood
Ken Rotcop / $16.95

Psychology for Screenwriters: Building Conflict in your Script
William Indick, Ph.D. / $26.95

Save the Cat! The Last Book on Screenwriting You'll Ever Need
Blake Snyder / $19.95

Screenwriting 101: The Essential Craft of Feature Film Writing
Neill D. Hicks / $16.95

Script Partners: What Makes Film and TV Writing Teams Work
Claudia Johnson and Matt Stevens / $24.95

The Script-Selling Game: A Hollywood Insider's Look at Getting Your Script Sold and Produced / Kathie Fong Yoneda / $14.95

Setting Up Your Shots: Great Camera Moves Every Filmmaker Should Know
Jeremy Vineyard / $19.95

Shaking the Money Tree, 2nd Edition: How to Get Grants and Donations for Film and Television / Morrie Warshawski / $26.95

Sound Design: The Expressive Power of Music, Voice, and Sound Effects in Cinema / David Sonnenschein / $19.95

Stealing Fire From the Gods: A Dynamic New Story Model for Writers and Filmmakers / James Bonnet / $26.95

Storyboarding 101: A Crash Course in Professional Storyboarding
James O. Fraioli / $19.95

The Ultimate Filmmaker's Guide to Short Films: Making It Big in Shorts
Kim Adelman / $14.95

What Are You Laughing At? How to Write Funny Screenplays, Stories, and More / Brad Schreiber / $19.95

The Working Director: How to Arrive, Thrive & Survive in the Director's Chair
Charles Wilkinson / $22.95

The Writer's Journey, 2nd Edition: Mythic Structure for Writers
Christopher Vogler / $24.95

The Writer's Partner: 1001 Breakthrough Ideas to Stimulate Your Imagination
Martin Roth / $19.95

Writing the Action Adventure: The Moment of Truth
Neill D. Hicks / $14.95

Writing the Comedy Film: Make 'Em Laugh
Stuart Voytilla and Scott Petri / $14.95

Writing the Fantasy Film: Heroes and Journeys in Alternate Realities
Sable Jak / $26.95

Writing the Killer Treatment: Selling Your Story Without a Script
Michael Halperin / $14.95

Writing the Second Act: Building Conflict and Tension in Your Film Script
Michael Halperin / $19.95

Writing the Thriller Film: The Terror Within
Neill D. Hicks / $14.95

DVD & VIDEOS

Hardware Wars: DVD
Written and Directed by Ernie Fosselius / $14.95

Hardware Wars: Special Edition VHS Video
Written and Directed by Ernie Fosselius / $9.95

Field of Fish: VHS Video
Directed by Steve Tanner and Michael Wiese, Written by Annamaria Murphy / $9.95